THE BARCLAYS GUIDE TO
Computing
for the Small Business

Barclays Small Business Series

Series Editors: Colin Gray and John Stanworth

This new series of highly practical books aimed at new and established small businesses has been written by carefully selected authors in conjunction with the Small Business Unit of Barclays Bank. All the authors have a wide experience of the theory and, more important, the *practice* of small business, and they address the problems that are likely to be encountered by new businesses in a clear and accessible way, including examples and case studies drawn from real business situations.

These comprehensive but compact guides will help owners and managers of small businesses to acquire the skills that are essential if they are to operate successfully in times of rapid change in the business environment.

The Barclays Guide to Marketing for the Small Business
Len Rogers

The Barclays Guide to Computing for the Small Business
Khalid Aziz

The Barclays Guide to International Trade for the Small Business
John Wilson

The Barclays Guide to Financial Management for the Small Business
Peter Wilson

The Barclays Guide to Managing Staff for the Small Business
Iain Maitland

The Barclays Guide to Growing the Small Business
Colin Gray

The Barclays Guide to Franchising for the Small Business
John Stanworth and Brian Smith

The Barclays Guide to Law for the Small Business
Stephen Lloyd

The Barclays Guide to Buying and Selling for the Small Business
John Gammon

THE BARCLAYS GUIDE TO
Computing
for the Small Business

KHALID AZIZ

BARCLAYS
Published by
BLACKWELL

Copyright © Khalid Aziz 1990

First published 1990

Basil Blackwell Ltd
108 Cowley Road, Oxford, OX4 1JF, UK

Basil Blackwell, Inc.
3 Cambridge Center
Cambridge, Massachusetts 02142, USA

All rights reserved. Except for the quotation of short passages for the purposes of criticism and review, no part of this publication may be reproduced, stored in a retrieval system, or transmitted, in any form or by any means, electronic, mechanical, photocopying, recording or otherwise, without the prior permission of the publisher.

Except in the United States of America, this book is sold subject to the condition that it shall not, by way of trade or otherwise, be lent, re-sold, hired out, or otherwise circulated without the publisher's prior consent in any form of binding or cover other than that in which it is published and without a similar condition including this condition being imposed on the subsequent purchaser.

British Library Cataloguing in Publication Data

A CIP catalogue record for this book is available from the British Library.

Library of Congress Cataloging in Publication Data

Aziz, Khalid.
The Barclays guide to computing for the small business / Khalid Aziz.
  p. cm. – (Barclays small business series)
ISBN 0–631–17255–6   ISBN 0–631–17256–4 (pbk.)
1. Small business – Data processing. I. Title. II. Series.
HF5548.2.A97 1990
658.02′2′0285 – dc20   89–29732 CIP

Typeset in 10½ on 12½pt Plantin
by Hope Services (Abingdon) Ltd
Printed in Great Britain by
T. J. Press Ltd, Padstow, Cornwall

For Kim

Contents

Foreword ix

Acknowledgement x

1 Introduction 1
Computers and business 1
Computer benefits 2
What this book will not tell you 4
What this book will do 5

2 Why computerize? 7
Computerize for profit 7
Assessing your business 8
Word processing: image and efficiency 13
Information gathering by computer: spreadsheets 15
1992 and all that: use of databases 17

3 What to computerize 20
Financial planning with spreadsheets 22
Word processing 32
Desktop publishing 34
Databases: filing on computer 36
Stock control 37
Future developments: networking and training 38

4 The software 41
What is software? 42
What software do you need? 42
Beware the complex package 44
Ease of use 44
Where will it lead? 46

Contents

How much will it cost?	47
Which package?	49

5 The hardware — 63
What you need to know about hardware	63
Beyond the jargon	66
Hardware – top of the pops	72
Choosing peripherals: monitors and printers	79
The second-hand option	84

6 Implementing the system — 86
Shall we tell the staff?	86
The outside consultant	90
Buying the system	92
Installation	98
Summary	106

7 Housing and security — 108
What kind of use?	108
Security	109

8 Training and monitoring — 116
Training	116
Monitoring	122

9 Expansion — 128
Knowing when and how to grow	128
Future trends	130
Be wise, be wary	133
Thoughts on the future	134

Appendix: Where to go for further advice — 136

Glossary — 139

Foreword

The last five years have seen a significant growth in the number of small businesses in all sectors of industry in the UK. Unfortunately they have also seen an increase in the numbers of problems encountered by those businesses. Often the problems could have been avoided with the right help and advice.

Barclays, in association with Basil Blackwell, is producing this series of guides to give that help and advice. They are comprehensive and written in a straightforward way. Each one has been written by a specialist in the field, in conjunction with Barclays Bank, and drawing on our joint expertise to ensure that the advice given is appropriate.

With the aid of these guides the businessman or woman will be better prepared to face the many challenges ahead, and, hopefully, will be better rewarded for their efforts.

George Cracknell
Director UK Business
Sector Services
Barclays Bank plc

Acknowledgement

Special thanks are due to my assistant, Amanda Whitehead, for her painstaking efforts with the typescript.

K. A.

1
Introduction

Computers and business

This book is aimed at two types of people in business. The first is someone who is just starting out in a business and wants to make sure that, wherever appropriate, computers are applied to those aspects of the business that could really benefit from computerization. For someone in a start-up situation the book aims to offer a guide to some of the real profit-making potential to be had from installing a computer system. It will try to help you make your mind up about the best kind of applications for your particular business. The second category of business person the book is aimed at is someone in a small and rapidly growing business who is finding it a strain to keep up with the pace and volume of business. Here computers can play a valuable part in enhancing the skills and efficiency of your existing staff and helping them cope better with the growing demands made on them.

Computers have been available to small businesses on a serious basis since the mid-1970s. In that time we have seen massive growth in the number of applications they can be put to. Not only that, the cost of computers – both hardware and software – has tumbled as the number of terminals and software programs has multiplied and the skills of the technologists in cramming more computing power on to one tiny silicon chip have grown. One telling way of illustrating how the cost of computers has fallen in real terms against their increase in power is to point out that that if the price of a Rolls-Royce had fallen at the same rate over the last twenty years, it would cost less than two pounds to purchase today!

All this means that computing power is within easy reach of virtually all businesses. The trouble is, with so much choice in a highly pressurized and competitive market, it is very easy to make the wrong decisions when considering computers for your business. A few years ago a survey carried out by the management consultancy division of a large firm of chartered accountants discovered that less than 50 per cent of business users were happy with the computer systems they had bought. In most cases systems had been purchased which turned out to be inappropriate for the business. The result of such unsatisfactory computer installations is often a drop in morale among staff having to operate the system and in all cases a loss of profitability. Much of that loss is hard to calculate at the time. The installation of computers can consume vast amounts of staff time which might otherwise be spent on more productive aspects of the business. It is therefore vital that you are sure you are going to get the best from the system once it is up and running. If the wrong set of decisions are taken, usually too quickly, the cost can be incalculable.

There are other computer issues which can potentially lose you money: the question of security, for example. There is at least one large company in the United States which simply never recovered from a fire which swept through its offices and destroyed all its computer records. No back-up copies had been made for safe keeping at another location. The company simply could not reinstate the records and without the records it could not provide its service to its customers. No customers, no cash flow, no business!

The moral of all this is that the person installing a computer system in a business for the first time carries a heavy burden of responsibility. It is very easy to make serious mistakes very early on if you are not clear on your objectives. Yet despite the potential downside risk associated with the installation of computer systems, there can be huge benefits if you get it right. These days a well thought out, efficient computer operation can make all the difference to the competitiveness of a business: the difference between make and break.

Computer benefits

For a small business a computer can be a godsend. It can make the difference between the success and failure of your operation. It can increase efficiency and boost profits. Computers can bring so many benefits to so many areas of business it is hard to know exactly where to begin. The secret is not to try to computerize everything all at once, but instead to take a cool look at the business and decide what parts of it really need computerizing.

All small businesses need to plan. However, planning is often an

Introduction

area which gets pushed to the bottom of the pile and neglected. A microcomputer using a spreadsheet package can help you forecast your financial needs. It can tell you the level of sales you will need to achieve to break even and produce targets for you to meet if you are to make real profits. It can show you the effect on the bottom line of taking on more staff or buying a new piece of equipment. Few businesses are too small to benefit from such planning and the beauty of it is you can do your planning without having to commit a penny of your capital – a real advantage in the pre-start-up phase of your business.

These days the image of a business, large or small, is increasingly important. A word processing package coupled with a high quality printer means that even the tiniest business can produce a clear and efficient image, whether it be on letters, price lists or even invoices; and it is an indisputable fact that this kind of professional image is increasingly becoming the expected norm in business communication today. Word processing can also make the drawing up of terms and documents containing complicated specifications much easier by calling up blocks of standard wording previously filed away on computer disk.

A database package storing customers' names and addresses can greatly improve a company's marketing effort. No longer does the launch of a new service or product have to be hit and miss. Having filed details of customers' spending records, it is easy to ask the computer to analyse what is being sold at what level and to whom. Such information generated in database reports can then be used as the basis for your marketing decisions. You can use both database and word processing to generate hundreds of personalized letters to mail out to prospective purchasers. Microcomputers make this level of business practice available to small businesses, whereas ten years ago only firms which could afford large mainframe computers could reap the benefits of such marketing efforts.

And using a computer to process orders can help improve the speed of response to your customers. As the business world grows increasingly competitive this speed of response factor will become more and more significant. If your customers cannot get the response they need from you when they want it they will go elsewhere; and if your marketing efforts generate a surge in custom it is vital that you are able to meet it. If you are in a service industry which requires a

Introduction

lot of estimating, a suitable computer program can greatly speed up the process of producing quotations. The quicker a quotation goes out, the faster, in theory at least, will your customer respond. In any event, the client should be impressed by the speed with which you turn the quotation around. Additionally, the faster you can do your quotations the more you can do and the more likely you are to fill your order book.

If you are in manufacturing you can use computers to monitor the speed and quality of production. You can keep tabs on stock and by careful, computer assisted monitoring reduce your stockholding, freeing up more cash for the business.

Above all, computers encourage a business to clean up its act. They demand efficient operating practices within the office. If you work in a muddle, the computer will only serve to speed up that muddle. Another potential pitfall is that if you are not disciplined in the way you use your computer system you can end up spending far too much time on the computer. It is very easy to waste a whole morning trying to troubleshoot an insignificant error. With proper planning you should be able to computerize simply without running the risk of taking large amounts of office time. Beware, too, as you computerize, the pitfall of concentrating too much power in the hands of just a few employees. If they leave or become disaffected you may find yourself with a computer nightmare on your hands. Of course, some people will have more aptitude for computers than others, but it is important to spread computer knowledge as widely as you can throughout your business.

What this book will not tell you

All businesses, even businesses in the same field, are different. They differ with the nature of the people running them and working within them. Some businesses are in such specialized areas that computers would be inappropriate, particularly in areas of low turnover, in terms of either volume or cash. For example, a master craftsman cabinet maker turning out say two pieces of high quality, highly priced furniture a year will hardly need a sophisticated computerized quality control package, or to use a computer to keep tabs of his stockholding of wood. However, he might want a computerized word processing system so that his letters to his valued and high calibre clients will have the same gloss as his products. In this instance it is easy to see that computer applications would not be appropriate for most parts of the business. In other businesses it is not so easy to differentiate between those parts of the operation which really justify computerization and those which do not. What this book will not do is attempt to make that decision for you. The decision to bring in a computer and decide which parts of the operation to computerize will always of necessity be yours. What this book will attempt to do is help you make that decision on a logical basis.

Similarly, this book will not shield you from all the pitfalls that await you as you start to computerize. It will point out some of the hazards, but as all businesses are different, you will find some difficulties peculiar to your business and your business alone. Sometimes they are difficult to discover until it is too late, but by understanding the issues at stake you will have a better chance of preventing a lot of disasters.

This book will not take decisions for you. If you have no knowledge of computers whatsoever there will have to be a 'back to school' element in the process if you are to get the best out of any computer system you eventually install. This book will help with that and will give you a grounding in the factors which you will have to consider if you are to get the best for your business from your computer system. The decisions, though will be yours, based on your experience and new-found knowledge.

What this book will do

The most important thing this book will do is help you ask the right questions. It is very easy when considering a computer system to take your eye off the ball and get side-tracked into issues which are not directly relevant to the business objectives you have set. This book will help you set those business objectives you want the computer to help you achieve. It will also help you ask the relevant questions geared to fulfilling those objectives. Such questions need to be asked of your staff and business partners, and, of course, of yourself. Less obvious, perhaps, will be the need to ask questions of

Introduction

your customers about how they feel about your proposed computerization. In some cases it may also be appropriate to ask questions of your suppliers. For example, if you have a major supplier you may want to consider a computer system which has the capacity to 'talk' to his computer.

After this consultative stage you should be able to formulate your business objectives. The next set of questions will be asked of the people attempting to sell you computer systems – both hardware and software. This book will help you translate your business objectives into a set of criteria for the software and ensure that the hardware you purchase will be capable of running that software to meet those criteria.

The next stage is to help you establish a 'critical path' to implement the computer system. This will involve laying down a time-scale with key events to be achieved over a given period. The critical path will have time blocked out for training staff to use the system. It will also make provision for ongoing training and set a time-table for phasing out the old manual systems.

Finally, the book will help you set parameters for monitoring the success of the computer installation and will give you some ideas about the sort of extra information you as a manager can demand from the system. This new information is one of the real but often hidden benefits of computerization. It can give you a real feel for how the business is going.

After all that you will be in a position to take the next step towards expanding the use of computers in your business and passing on the benefits of increased efficiency. There is a great deal to be considered and most people in business are short of time. However, if you are to avoid some of the disasters that have befallen businesses which in the past have tried to install computers too hastily, you will have to make time. There are benefits to be reaped; but only if great care is taken at the early stages.

Ten years ago very few small businesses would even consider installing a microcomputer system. Today for many it would be unthinkable that they could operate without one. Much depends on the type and size of an individual business, but there is no doubt that most businesses can benefit in some degree from a microcomputer. The secret is to choose wisely. I hope this book will help.

2

Why computerize?

> **Outline**
>
> This chapter assesses the need to computerize. We look at:
> - computerizing for profit
> - how to assess the reasons for computerizing your business
> - the role of word processors
> - the purpose of spreadsheets
> - the implications of the emergence of The Single European Market

In this chapter we will look at the fundamental reasons for computerization. Many businesses do not absolutely need to install a computer. Certainly it is unlikely that they will need to computerize all of their operations. This chapter will help you test your assumptions about the world of computers and what they can do for you and your business. If after reading it you decide that a computer is not for you, all well and good. You will have saved yourself a lot of time and effort, not to mention cost in terms of both cash and the hidden costs of diverting productive time to cope with the installation of computer systems. You may, on the other hand, have a clearer idea of how a computer *could* serve your business.

Computerize for profit

There can be only one paramount reason for taking any major business decision and that is to improve profitability. Sometimes such improvements take time to come through to the bottom line, but there has to be a clear understanding that sooner or later the profit will come through. When considering computerization it is often easy to overlook this prime objective. Throughout your decision making process you must ensure you do not lose sight of this overall aim.

The factors which affect profitability fall broadly into two groups. First there are those factors which directly affect profit, such as sales and cost of supplies. Then there are the secondary factors, such as improved efficiency in producing management accounts or keeping on top of PAYE payments. When considering installing computers into your business you need to understand which areas will benefit directly from the computer operation and which might be only slightly affected. In reality it will probably not be as clear cut as it may seem at first, and there will be shades of grey when you consider which areas of business will best benefit from the computer.

Assessing your business

So how do you set about examining your business to assess the likely areas for computerization? A good starting point is the so-called 'SWOT' analysis which you may be more familiar with as a marketing tool. SWOT stands for Strengths, Weaknesses, Opportunities and Threats. In the main Strengths and Weaknesses are factors within your business or *internal* factors, while Opportunities and Threats are issues outside your business or *external* factors. It is self-evident that you will have more control over the internal factors than the external ones. However, it may well be that computerization will answer more of the external factors than the internal ones. At this stage it is as well to keep an open mind. What needs to be done now is to draw up an honest SWOT analysis. You may have already done this in connection with a marketing operation. If so, have another look at it and see if it still stands up to detailed scrutiny. Remember, it must be accurate and honest. It is the basis on which you are going to make a series of key decisions in your business, committing several thousand pounds and hundreds of hours of your time and that of your staff.

Exhibit 1 is a SWOT analysis for a company which manufactures and erects conservatories. This example is by no means comprehensive but it serves to illustrate how we would consider the computer issues in this particular business. The first point to come out of the analysis is the fact that we are dealing with a thriving company with a strong

Why computerize?

Strengths	Weaknesses	Opportunities	Threats
Established	Old image	Growing market	Competition
Good product	Quality	1992: Single	Imports
Skilled workers	Worker shortage	European Market	
Good management	Poor information		
Market leader	Up to capacity		

Exhibit 1

cash flow. It is well established in the market place with a good product produced by skilled workers who are managed professionally. This has given the company a market lead. Obviously there are firms which are not in such a strong position but which still use computers, but there is a firm first rule which applies to all businesses:

Before you consider bringing in a computer system, be sure you can afford it.

Obviously, for start-up businesses and those at the survival phase of development the question is rather a different one, but even then installing a computer is an investment which will need funding. In our conservatory business things look good, but as everyone knows in business, nothing stays the same for ever. If the business does not progress it will go backwards. It could stand to lose its market share. One of its weaknesses is that it suffers from a stuffy image which does not attract the newer purchasers of conservatories. Part of that image is tied up with the way it deals with potential customers. Most of the estimating is done by 'old George' who has been doing a very good job for years. The trouble is, George has his own way of working which he is reluctant to share with anyone else. But what happens if George falls under a bus? Who will take over then? This is obviously a major threat to the operation. Not only that, but even if George is spared the attentions of a number nine bus, his way of working is painfully slow by modern standards, especially when compared with some of the newer entrants to the conservatory market. It takes our company up to three weeks to produce a drawing and quotation for each job. Some companies are getting drawings and firm quotes to potential customers within days. How are they doing it? With the help of computers, of course!

Why computerize?

The faster drawings and quotations are sent out, the quicker customers can make up their minds and the quicker business comes in. The trouble is, as we see from our SWOT analysis, the factory is already up to capacity, there is a shortage of skilled workers and quality is beginning to suffer. George knows this. He is happy with the way he does his job and like most people is resistant to change. However, the management knows that if they are to keep their position as market leader something has to be done. The question is, what to do first and how?

Perhaps the obvious thing to do is to copy the competition and install a computer capable of turning out drawings quickly. Quite often keeping up with the competition appears to be one of the most compelling reasons for installing some kind of computer system, but such reasoning needs careful examination. In the case of our conservatory company using computers to speed up the process of estimating and drawing could spell disaster. Even if it had the desired effect it would simply create more orders leading to even bigger delays. The pressure would be on the workforce to produce more, faster, and quality would deteriorate yet further, leading to an increasing number of customers becoming disgruntled with having to wait longer for an inferior product.

We have to look at the fundamental external problems facing the business. Let us look at the Threats. There is increasing competition and there are imports of cheap ready-made conservatories of reasonable quality. There is little we can do about these Threats, but nevertheless they should not be ignored. It is always good to keep an eye on what the competition is up to. As for the imports, the key factor here is to ensure that the quality of our products is far higher than that of the cheaper imports.

Looking at the Opportunities, the market is still growing apace; we are serving the burgeoning leisure industry. With the creation of the Single European Market by 1992 the company is well placed to sell into the rest of Europe. Clearly the problem is one of capacity. The way to increase capacity would be either to expand the existing premises or move to a new location with more space. Both routes will involve taking on more staff and investing in extra equipment. A physical move to bigger premises will also involve considerable management time and effort. So let us see if we cannot improve the efficiency of our existing operation.

The secret to this lies in the issue of quality. What seems to be happening on the shop floor of our conservatory factory is that somehow the measurements carefully taken on site and then transferred to drawings sometimes get garbled. This results in panels and in some cases whole conservatories not fitting properly when they are delivered on site for erection. Sometimes the panels can be 'hammered to fit', as they say in the building trade, but usually a completely new panel has to be made, and occasionally the entire conservatory has to be scrapped and made again. As the customer is not best pleased with this, the particular conservatory now becomes a crisis and pushes other work in the factory back. The effect is total disruption of the production process, yet more delays to other customers and a demoralized workforce, with the shop floor workers blaming George the estimator and his sales team, and George blaming those lazy good-for-nothing loafers in the factory.

The costs involved in putting right faulty products are not easy to calculate. Many businesses do not even try to quantify them. It is clear, however, that in our conservatory business quality is an issue which is affecting capacity and if quality could be improved then we could increase capacity. Quality is a primary factory when it comes to improving profitability on the bottom line. How could computers help in this instance?

Consider what happens at the moment. George goes and measures up. He writes the measurements in a notebook which he gives to a clerk in the drawing office to type up. Assuming George writes them down correctly in the first place here is the first area where mistakes may be made. Once the figures are typed up, they go to a draughtsman together with instructions about the type of conservatory required. The figures are transferred to the drawing board, another opportunity for mistakes to be made. Once the drawing is approved by the customer, the drawing office draws up a list of new measurements for the manufacture of the conservatory panels: a third potential point at which mistakes can be made. The measurements are read by the factory workers and translated into settings for the machinery. Here again mistakes can be made. So we see that (excluding the possibility of George making a mistake in the first place) there is a total of four stages at which the figures can become mixed up. When you consider the mass of measurements

Why computerize?

required in the manufacturing process of a conservatory it is probably surprising there are not more mistakes!

Does it take a computer to sort out the problem? In theory, it should not. Everyone should be encouraged to be more painstaking and diligent. However, we are dealing with human fallibility and this is where a computer comes in. Using a Computer Aided Design – known as CAD – system George could enter his measurements into a portable, hand held computer plugged into the main computer back at the office. This CAD system could then draw the conservatory to scale and produce a list of measurements and settings for the production machinery. By combining the Computer Aided Design with a Computer Aided Manufacturing – or CAM – system that list of measurements and settings could be transferred electronically to the shop floor machinery. All of this cuts out the four identified areas of potential error. However, the burden of accuracy now all rests on George and it would be prudent to insert somewhere in the system a means by which the measurements are checked. Probably the best point would be once customer approval has been obtained, before going ahead with the manufacturing process.

Of course it may well turn out that all along it was George getting his measurements wrong in the first place. If that is the case and you simply introduce an extra measurements check, quality ought to increase and that will have been achieved without the aid of the computer. The point of saying this is to illustrate that in fact computers *in themselves* do not usually create improvements. What they do is speed up the systems to which they are applied. If the systems are wrong all you will do is create a bigger mess more quickly.

It is tempting to use computers to try to sort out problems. This is a mistake and leads to even greater complications. The problems have to be sorted out manually first before handing them over to the computer. It is far better to computerize the areas you are doing well in, as this will lead to greater efficiency. However, there are other areas in our conservatory company which we could tackle. Back to the SWOT analysis.

Let us look at this question of image. The company is well established. It goes back more than fifty years, in fact. The trouble is that its catalogue, its letterheads, its invoices all reflect this. In the past the market for conservatories was peopled principally by older couples who had made enough money over a number of years to afford what they regarded as one of life's little luxuries. To them a conservatory was part of the fulfilment of a lifetime ambition. Nowadays much younger couples, finding themselves affluent earlier, make up the largest section of the conservatory market. To them a conservatory is just one of a long string of luxury purchases. But our company's image just does not address this market sector and we are left with an old image projecting to an old and declining sector of the market. If we do not do something, we stand to lose our dominance as market leader.

A further crucial point is that many of the newer entrants to the conservatory market have come from a background of double glazing sales and are noted for their aggressive marketing and sales techniques. They are faster at getting their foot in the door and quicker at closing the sale. They are certainly far more adept at turning the sale around. They issue estimates and quotations within days whereas it takes our company weeks. However, the new firms still have the same problems we have when it comes to delivery and quality. We have already discussed what we might do about quality, so we know we can improve that and therefore get closer to ensuring prompt delivery. We are left, then, with the problem of what to do about the company's image.

Word processing: image and efficiency

One of the quickest and simplest ways to improve a company's image using computers is to install a *word processing* system. At a stroke you can transform the way a company looks on paper. There is no longer any excuse for letters to be sent out with spelling mistakes or typing errors: not only is it easy to correct mistakes before they are printed out on to paper, but most word processing programs come with additional software to allow you to check the spelling of words. You will also be able to store standard letters and pieces of text to use when sending out quotations, chasing up bad debts and so on. This facility to produce good letters with ease will inevitably increase the use of the written word to communicate with customers and suppliers, but this is no bad thing. It will make the

Why computerize?

running of your operation more businesslike and there is no substitute for having a letter to refer to to settle a dispute over what was said and when.

Word processing does not stop there. It can help you update price lists without having to resort to a printer. In the past, firms were reluctant to re-issue price lists to keep pace with costs because of the time and effort involved. Our conservatory company, for example, lowers its prices for the winter period to stimulate demand for conservatories at a time when they are not uppermost in people's minds. Like many other firms, they have invested heavily in a glossy, four colour brochure illustrating their products. A separate price list is inserted loose in the brochure, and this is updated from time to time but currently no more than twice a year. The trouble is that because of the time and effort involved in having the price list typeset and printed the company tends to hold on until a number of increases in costs have come through before reprinting the list.

All of this costs money and erodes the company's margins. On average our conservatory firm reprints its price list just twice a year. This means that it stands to carry increases in its costs without passing them on to its customers for up to six months at a time. By having the price list stored on its word processing system it is a simple matter to change prices as costs rise. All this takes no more than minutes and can be done in-house, thus eliminating the delays of having to go through a typesetter and printer. If necessary our company could issue new price lists every month – or even once a week!

Word processing is a great help to a business because, in addition to improving a company's image, it also helps people working within the business to 'get it down on paper'. Too often in small businesses people do not formulate their ideas properly and rely solely on what is in their head to carry them through. The people who do well in steady sustained businesses are those who think things through and put their ideas down on paper. Only then can they be scrutinized and tested to see if they stand up. One of the most important areas here is management information.

Why computerize?

Information gathering by computer: spreadsheets

If we look at the SWOT analysis for our conservatory company we can see that we have good management who know their business and are able to get the best out of the workforce. However, it appears they have only poor information to go on. What do we mean by that? Quite often a management does not know it has poor information until it is pointed out by an outsider, usually their accountant or business adviser. Let us consider what should happen in a well run business.

Each month there should be a board meeting of the directors. In the case of a sole trader or a partnership they will not, of course, be directors as such but it is important that some kind of meeting takes place. Even the sole trader should consider this, however ludicrous the idea of a meeting with himself might appear. Time should be set aside to consider the business's performance. At this monthly meeting there are a number of key factors which need to be considered. What is the cash position of the business at the bank? How have sales been during the previous month? What are the projections for the current month and those beyond? How will projected sales affect the cash required to fund the manufacturing process? How has the manufacturing side of the business been going? How many poor quality returns of product have there been? All these are fundamental questions about the health of the business. All of them require the collection and collation of detailed information. Before computers this had to be done manually and required large numbers of support staff to produce the figures. The result of this was that only the largest companies dealing with big numbers in production and sales could afford to gather such information. Smaller concerns had to content themselves with struggling on in the dark. Even the big firms which could afford to have such a large part of their workforce engaged on the gathering of management information had to content themselves with the information being weeks out of date by the time it could be considered at a board meeting. Today all that has changed.

Using computers, companies can gather management information in a fraction of the time it used to take and with a fraction of the staff. Additionally, such information is not restricted to large

Why computerize?

companies. Even the smallest business can use microcomputers to help it gather and collate valuable information which will help it make better decisions about the way it is going.

Before the advent of microcomputers, board meetings were seldom held less than two weeks after the month end. Nowadays it is possible to hold meetings and have all the information available in a matter of days after the end of the month. All thanks to computers. How would the ability to use such information apply to our conservatory company? Let us look at quality. Although the production director keeps a close eye on how production is going on a day to day basis, it really does help to have the figures for overall output, reject panels, returned conservatories, wastage, etc. crystallized and clearly presented every month so that the entire board of the company can see what the overall picture is. It may well be that new machinery is needed. The performance of this machinery will need to be monitored. This too needs to be analysed and computers can help in this. Similarly, sharp increases in the costs of sales, raw materials, overtime, etc. need to be monitored and carefully controlled. One of the biggest traps into which a growing company can fall is overtrading. What this means is that the company takes on more and more business in the form of orders without due regard for how it is going to pay for the raw materials required for the extra production, given that it can take months for customers to pay. In this situation the company can very easily run out of cash and reach the limit of its borrowing power. Using a computer program to project forward the effect of sales on the cash position will help the board of directors ease up on sales if it looks as though the company will run out of money. The use of simple *spreadsheet* programs can help even the smallest of businesses analyse the past and plan the future.

All this may sound daunting. In fact the provision of good management information, once you have got to grips with the computer, can be simplicity itself. Initially the setting up of a spreadsheet can be time consuming, but once set up it requires relatively small amounts of information each month to provide real information. The next chapter will explain how it works in practice.

Why computerize?

1992 and all that: use of databases

In the Opportunities column of our SWOT analysis we have stated that the market is still growing and that the creation of the Single European Market will also provide new impetus to the business. Our conservatory company is situated on the south coast of England. By 1992 its domestic market of 60 million people in the UK will shoot up to 320 million people throughout Europe. The company is well established and is well placed to take advantage of these developments. However, it will need to make strenuous efforts to keep in touch with its market. There are a number of ways of doing this. One is by advertising, another is through public relations, a third is by direct mail. A computer can be of real assistance for the last two of these. The company could, for example, prepare a circular letter to launch its new range of conservatories together with suitable copy to send out to 'lifestyle' magazines such as *Homes and Gardens* and *Good Housekeeping* which, although published in England, are widely read in continental Europe. To do this efficiently the names of the garden editors of the various magazines together with the addresses of their publishers need to be gathered and collated. This can be done most efficiently using a computerized *database* system.

Such databases can also be used to log existing customers. As new products are brought out, such customers (assuming they have been satisfied the first time) serve as a useful base for a product launch. Similarly, if the company wished to launch its conservatories in, say, France, it could have its public relations company translate its press releases, input them into the word processor and use them for a direct mail-shot to French magazines. Again, if the company wanted to mail directly to potential conservatory customers in, say, a thirty-mile radius of Calais, it could do this by buying a list of names and addresses from a reputable agency which could be supplied on computer disk for direct inputting into its database system.

One aspect of the Single European Market is the impact of new legislation coming out of Brussels affecting in particular the standards used when making products. No firm can expect to be unaffected by these and it is important for companies wanting to do

Why computerize?

business in Europe, either now or in the future, to keep pace with developments. This will ensure that a company does not find itself out on a limb with a product it cannot sell because it does not conform to European standards. One way of keeping pace with this is to tap into one of the European databases which are now available. If you own a microcomputer you can do this using a device known as a *modem* which will help connect the computer to the database. The Department of Trade and Industry run a database called Spearhead which can be accessed in this way. Chartered accountants and business advisers Deloitte, Haskins & Sells also operate a European database which has the added advantage that it can be searched by subject. So our conservatory company could call up the database and ask for information on the legislation affecting the construction of conservatories in European Community countries. In this way the firm can keep abreast of developments as they happen and reduce the risk of being wrong-footed by changes in the law.

In the case of our conservatory company we have established some key rules of thumb when it comes to considering the question 'Why computerize?'. To answer the question we have had to consider the strengths and weaknesses of the company and the threats and opportunities it faces. We have seen how computers might help with all of these, but we have also realized that it is useless to computerize a manual system which is already in a mess: much better to look at computerizing something which is already working well for the business. It is unlikely that any business will not be able to gain something out of installing a computer. The crucial question is just how much its profitability will be enhanced by doing so. Occasionally it may well be that the business has to computerize to keep pace with the competition. If, however, you feel the benefits of computerization will not bring added profit to your operations then you simply should not go ahead.

Key points Why computerize?

- Ask yourself: 'Can I afford to computerize?'
- Conduct a SWOT analysis for your business
- Identify areas ripe for computerization
- Do not computerize bad manual systems
- Computerize for profit
- If in doubt do not computerize

3
What to Computerize

Outline

This chapter looks at the implications of computerization in a little more detail. We consider:

- the role of spreadsheets in financial planning
- graphics
- invoicing
- accounts procedures
- word processing
- desktop publishing
- storing and using databases
- controlling stock
- future trends

In this chapter we will look in a little more depth at the range of business applications a computer can be used for and try to help you to assess which applications are most suited to your business. All businesses have different needs, but the overriding rule should be to computerize those parts of the business which will help you improve overall profitability. This may not necessarily happen in the short term, but increasing profit through computers should certainly be a long-term goal.

First, a little background on the world of computers. There are three main types of computer. *Mainframes* are large computers with extremely big memories which until a decade or so ago were the only types of computer available to business. They cost hundreds of thousands of pounds, sometimes millions of pounds. *Minicomputers* cost tens of thousands of pounds and are used for the more complex business applications such as fully integrated stockholding and invoicing programs. The cost of *microcomputers* can be measured in thousands of pounds and this book concentrates on the various uses to which they can be put for business. The principal difference between

What to computerize

mainframes, minicomputers and microcomputers is one of capacity. By and large, microcomputers can tackle the same range of applications but have difficulty in handling large amounts of complex data. However, these computers have revolutionized business and there is little doubt that used properly they provide great value for money.

There is a whole range of highly imaginative and sophisticated applications for microcomputers in the world of business. In the early days of microcomputing there was a tendency for software writers to produce solutions for problems which did not really exist. Nowadays software development has settled down and the packages being produced today are not only more relevant to business but much easier for the non-computer-literate business user to put into operation.

Some businesses have very specialized needs which call for very specific computer programs, many of which would have to be specially written, but there is a broad range of activities common to most businesses on which there are plenty of packages to choose from. The secret is to identify the areas which will help your business best and sort them into an order of priority, remembering that it would be foolish to attempt to computerize everything at once.

One drawback which it is as well to face is that sitting in front of a computer playing with plans and figures takes time, the one thing in short supply for most people in business (apart from cash to develop the business!). Time spent closeted with the computer is arguably time that might be better spent elsewhere – on the shop floor, perhaps, geeing up morale; on the phone, bringing in new business; out and about making new contacts. Even if you do not neglect those areas of the business, the people who will really pay the price for time lost to the computer could well be your family. You do need to consider how much time you are going to allow yourself to spend on your microcomputer. To many people it can become something of a 'bug' and they find themselves glued to the computer screen for hours on end. The secret is to make the computer work for you in the areas which really matter and not to get side-tracked into non-profitable areas. Having said that, owning a microcomputer starts most people off on a voyage of discovery and opens up a whole new world which many find difficult to resist!

Let us look at the areas which could spell extra profit for your business.

What to computerize

Financial planning with spreadsheets

Many people argue that before the advent of the business microcomputer, most small businesses had hardly heard of financial planning, apart perhaps from the plan submitted to the bank to support a loan application. If the plan happened at all it was done by the accountant. Now there is no excuse for this, because every business computer makes great claims for the range of financial planning packages which can be run on it with total ease.

On closer examination it is perhaps a little difficult to understand what all the fuss is about. Often the first use of a computer in a small business is in producing the cash flows and budgets required for the business plan in the pre-start-up phase. Before the advent of microcomputers these had to be done by hand with all the individual calculations laboriously worked out. Invariably, because of the sheer difficulty of producing the information and keeping it updated, there was little attention to cash flow forecasts and businesses relied on a policy of 'muddling through' often with disastrous results. These days there is no excuse for not having good information; installing a microcomputer provides an easy and streamlined means of financial planning.

Sales can be recorded, invoices produced, statements compiled. Management can keep track of the current state of payments from customers in relation to goods despatched. Regular printouts of aged debtors, that, people who have owed you money for more than the period allowed in your terms of business (usually thirty days) can be had. All this helps you guard against strain on your company's cash flow. A computer can help you keep track of your bills and take full advantage of credit terms by reminding you when it is time to pay.

One aspect of financial planning revolves around the setting up of what is known as a spreadsheet – a series of columns into which figures are inserted to correspond to income and expenditure on, usually, a month by month basis. The beauty of doing it on a computer is that you can quite literally play about with the figures. When just one figure is changed, the rest of the figures in the spreadsheet are automatically amended by the computer to correspond with the different input. This enables you to play 'what if?' games with your business. The possibilities can be quite amusing, if somewhat in the realms of fantasy: 'What if I treble my turnover and double my gross profit margin?!'

The use of a financial planning spreadsheet can have distinct advantages. No serious business people can really afford to be without some idea about where they are trying to take the business. Spreadsheets can be used to set up financial targets for both profit and loss accounts and cash flow forecasts and analysis. As the real figures come in they can be inserted against those in the budget. Month by month you, as manager of your business, can get an accurate assessment of how you are performing against any given targets. Bank managers can often be impressed by this – assuming the figures are going the right way!

If you look at the sample spreadsheet in Exhibit 2 you can see that the entire financial expenditure and income for a business covering a period of seven months are laid out on one piece of paper. In practice the spreadsheet usually covers a period of twelve months; we have used seven months for ease of illustration. For each month there are two columns: one for a predicted or *budget* figure – that is, the receipts and payments we expect to make – and one for the *actual* figures as they turn out each month. The figures are entered on to the spreadsheet at the end of each month in preparation for the board meeting. You will see that actual figures have been entered right up to May – a very bad month for sales! However, things are predicted to pick up again in July and August. The question is: 'What if they don't?'

The spreadsheet illustrated is for a business struggling to survive. You will see that if you deduct the cost of sales from the payments made each month the business is costing between £4,000 and £7,000 to run, even if it does not sell a thing. That figure, although it changes somewhat from month to month, is known as the company's *fixed costs*. Fixed costs include everything which is not a direct result of making a sale. You can see that the cash held at the bank is in fact a negative figure, which means that the company is being kept afloat by its overdraft facility – in this case to a limit of £70,000. The prediction is that for July the overdraft at £68,426 will come perilously close to its limit. The board of directors, looking at this at their early June board meeting, will want to ensure that costs do not rise and will look at the payments to see if there is some way

What to computerize

1st June-A	Budget	FEBRUARY Actual	Budget	MARCH Actual	Budget	APRIL Actual	Budget	MAY Actual	Budget	JUNE Actual	Budget	JULY Actual	Budget	AUGUST Actual
RECEIPTS														
Sales	17897.00	17312.00	5251.00	466.76	4063.97	4065.47	0.00	0.00	845.00		14000.00		11000.00	
Services	2684.55	2596.80	787.65	70.01	511.38	511.38	0.00	0.00	370.00		350.00		1650.00	
VAT Output	50.00	73.86	20.00	536.77	609.60	686.29	0.00	0.00	182.25		2152.50			
Directors Loan						99.74								
TOTAL RECEIPTS A	20631.55	19982.66	6038.65	536.77	5184.95	5362.88	0.00	0.00	1397.25	0.00	16502.50	0.00	12650.00	0.00
PAYMENTS														
Cost of sales	5800.00	2079.60	11868.04	9601.55	7501.10	1313.48	8234.90	6371.9	1000.00		2700.00		5200.00	
Stock purchases			0.00	4.02										
R and D purchases	250.00	0.00	335.00	20.00	335.00	342.50		556.00						
Capital Expenditure	1086.04	0.00	1086.04	815.01	271.04	271.04			650.00					
Tools and equipment	10.00		20.00	32.00	20.00			43.47			45.00			
Directors' Remuneratio	999.93	999.93	1000.00	1004.73	1004.73	1004.73	1000.00	1004.23	1003.96		1000.00		1000.00	
Employees	328.00	267.20	204.00	122.15	923.00	892.44	800.00	618.00	620.00		750.00		1348.00	
Manufacturing costs	100.00	100.00	90.00	50.00	40.00		50.00	100.00	100.00		120.00			
PAYE	1369.45	1369.45	350.00	0.00	950.16	1077.98	540.00	0.00	1299.83		540.00		800.00	
Directors' Expenses	60.00	50.28	60.00	64.35	60.00	24.14	60.00		60.00		60.00		60.00	
Consultants' Expenses	97.00	88.60	30.00	29.50	60.00	50.60	30.00	32.06	30.00		30.00		30.00	
Insurance	237.00	263.35	100.00	90.20	75.00	58.30	75.00	35.70	75.00		75.00		75.00	
Power and heat	20.00	30.00	20.00	0.00	20.00	20.00	60.00	40.00	20.00		20.00		20.00	
Telephone					348.78	303.29					350.00			
Printing and stationer	60.00	22.35	345.00	411.96	50.00	1.43	50.00		50.00		50.00		50.00	
Legal and audit	950.00	950.00	260.00	260.00			62.25		713.00					
Computer sundries	35.00	20.53	40.00	54.04	50.00	5.49	80.00		50.00		50.00		50.00	
Mags/subscrip	20.00	21.06	5.00	1.30	10.00		5.00		10.00		5.00		10.00	
Advertising/PR	39.60	0.00	54.00	0.00	39.60		54.00	50.57	0.00		54.00		0.00	
Exhibitions	467.23	0.00	467.23	467.23	1510.00	1510.00		21.85						
Courses/training														
Commission														
Carriage and postage	50.00	32.32	50.00	57.96	50.00	13.73	30.00	25.70	50.00		50.00		50.00	
Vehicle Expenses	170.00	196.60	160.00	173.11	160.00	156.13	160.00	89.19	160.00		160.00		160.00	
Entertainment	20.00	22.35	40.00	51.10	20.00	17.02	50.00		50.00		50.00		50.00	
Repairs and renewals	20.00	9.80	20.00	40.01	28.51	42.51	50.00		50.00		50.00		50.00	
Sundries	50.00	42.47	50.00	13.77	50.00	36.40	50.00	9.35	50.00		50.00		50.00	
Loan repayments	134.57	134.57	134.57	134.57	134.57	134.57	134.57	134.57	134.57		134.57		134.57	
Bank interest			1400.00	1420.63					1400.00					
Bank charges			100.00	168.20		200.00			100.00					
Repay Directors' loan	203.85	203.85	73.86	73.86	0.00	0.00	99.74	99.74						
VAT input	893.39	471.27	2208.20	1366.45	1630.68	618.02	1316.42	1069.07	417.45		1119.60		843.00	
VAT returns	-1235.71	-1268.71							1750.75					
TOTAL PAYMENTS B	12235.35	6106.87	21470.94	16527.70	15342.17	8093.80	12991.88	10251.40	9844.56		11363.17		9980.57	
Cash inflow/outflow (A	8396.20	13875.79	-15432.29	-15990.93	-10157.22	-2730.92	-12991.88	-10251.40	-8447.31		5139.33		2669.43	
Opening bank balance	-44881.96	-44881.96	-31006.17	-31006.17	-46997.10	-46997.10	-49728.02	-49728.02	-59979.42		-68426.73		-63287.40	
Closing bank balance	-36485.76	-31006.17	-46438.46	-46997.10	-57154.32	-49728.02	-62719.90	-59979.42	-68426.73		-63287.40		-60617.97	

What to computerize

of cutting down on expenditure. Looking at the spreadsheet, where could cuts be made?

Entertainment is budgeted at £50 per month. Looking back through the spreadsheet at previous months it seems that the directors have been very careful on this front and have kept well within budget. In any event £50 is neither here nor there when it comes to an overdraft approaching £70,000. There is a figure of £713 budgeted for Legal and Audit. In fact this is their accountants' fee for auditing and completing the firm's company returns. If things get tough they could always talk to their accountants and ask them to wait for payment. Most accountancy firms would be understanding on this, at least for a month or two. There is £650 in the budget for Tools and Equipment. This clearly is expenditure which could wait, but not if it will affect the delivery of products to customers. £1,300 is budgeted to go out in June on PAYE. Perhaps we could hold on to that? PAYE and VAT are areas where small businesses often try to hold back payments. Frequently they come unstuck. You can be charged interest on late payment of PAYE and if you pay your VAT returns late you get sent automatically (via a computer!) what is known as a Statutory Liability Notice or SLN. If you are a persistent late payer the Customs and Excise impose swingeing penalties which can cost a firm dearly. In any event no one will want to attract the attention of either the Revenue or the Customs. Investigations, even if you have nothing to hide, can be time consuming and costly. So if our directors are sensible they will not consider holding back on PAYE or VAT payments.

We can see from this spreadsheet that there is little scope for cutting costs unless we lay off staff or stop paying the directors. What we need is a substantial boost to sales. Even this could be tricky. If sales grow too quickly we run the risk of overtrading, discussed in the previous chapter – when we run out of money to fund the purchase of raw materials to make the products we need to sell.

So our board of directors will need to continue on a steady path of controlled sales growth coupled with tightly monitored costs. As long as we make our sales targets of £14,000 and £11,000 in July and August we should be all right, with the overdraft coming down steadily. But with our fixed costs running at the rate of around £5,000 a month we have just two months' breathing space before we go through our overdraft limit. So we have to continue to increase our sales and control our costs.

This scenario is not untypical for many small, struggling firms. Using a computer spreadsheet to analyse cash flowing into and out of the business does not in itself make things better. What it does do is present in stark reality where the business is going. We can manipulate the figures on the spreadsheet to establish what level of sales we need to avoid disaster. We can also use the spreadsheet to project forward to find out when, if we carry on the way we are, the business will come into profit. Indeed, the spreadsheet also serves to tell us when, if we carry on the way we are, we will finally have to shut up shop and admit defeat! In either case the computer will have offered us the chance of doing something to change the trend. None of the information on a spreadsheet is any substitute for good judgement. The data on a spreadsheet will simply help *you* make the tough decisions about your business. The ease with which figures can be inserted into a spreadsheet will help you make those decisions earlier rather than later.

Spreadsheets into graphics

Many people find it difficult to interpret masses of figures, especially when they are trying to draw conclusions about general trends. It is possible, using special software associated with spreadsheet packages, to translate hard figures into graphs and charts. These charts can take many forms but the most popular are *line charts*, in which a single line links various points over a period of time, usually months; *bar charts* or *histograms*, where data is displayed in columns of varying heights; and the *pie chart*, so called because it takes the form of a circular 'pie' cut into wedges of varying size to represent sectors of a business operation.

Line charts are typically used to show monthly sales figures. By plotting the business's fixed costs month by month it is possible to see at a glance when the company is breaking even and what level of profit or loss there is. You can also use line charts to plot how accurate your budgeting has been. If the 'actual' line is consistently below the predicted 'budget' line you will know that you have been over-optimistic. It is also important that you are not too pessimistic with your budgeting. If you are you will not be taking best advantage of profits generated by a higher than predicted level of business, profits that could be used for further investment to expand the business. Optimistic or pessimistic, either way, while the knowledge of how accurate you are in budgeting might not necessarily be usefully available to you in the start-up phase of the business it will be helpful as you expand your business and start to budget for subsequent years. The ability to budget accurately, using this historical knowledge of the way your business operates from month to month, from season to season, will greatly assist you when you are putting together a case for borrowing money from the bank or seeking to introduce new equity funding to your company. Potential backers will always be more impressed with the business that can clearly demonstrate that its corporate finger is on the pulse of its operations.

Bar charts are popular for displaying comparative figures. For each month you have two columns side by side showing this year's figures against last year's. An alternative method of using bar charts allows the various elements which make up the cost of supply to be illustrated. Thus the first part of the column shows raw material costs, the next part manufacturing costs, the next packaging, the next delivery, and so on. This is useful when monitoring the performance of various products and again helps management to see at a glance how well they have been progressing on improving efficiency and driving down costs. Pie charts are typically used to show where money is being spent on a sector by sector basis. They are a handy way of getting an overview of how individual parts of a business relate to each other in terms of spending. Graphics are particularly useful when management wishes to get a proper overview of the situation without getting bogged down with the minute detail of exactly which sums of money are being spent where. The use of colour in a graphics system enhances this ability to make comparative judgements by enabling you to see the 'big picture' more clearly.

It is important to be clear that they are a presentational tool rather than a functional tool like the spreadsheet itself; but none the less, where presentation is of the essence, whether internally or externally, they can add a great deal. If you are considering using a graphics package you must ensure that it is compatible with your spreadsheet software. If you find you have to transfer figures via a

What to computerize

keyboard to a graphics program it is debatable whether the extra time involved is justified by the enhanced facility to make a proper analysis of the figures. Most small businesses simply cannot afford the extra time. A graphics package which is integrated with a spreadsheet program is ideal and should enable you to display figures graphically at the touch of just a few keys. However, if you opt for such an integrated package you will almost certainly need a more powerful computer and this, together with the increased cost of the integrated software, will add to your system costs. Remember too that if you opt for a graphics program which offers you a colour display you will incur more costs again, with far more computer memory being required plus a colour monitor for your visual display unit. If you want to print out your graphics in colour, a colour printer can cost you far more than the original computer system itself!

Invoicing with spreadsheets

In a small business a spreadsheet package can be made use of for a very simple but otherwise tedious business function, that of issuing invoices. Let us take, say, a plumber. His charges fall into very specific areas. Firstly there is his fixed minimum call out charge; then there is his hourly rate; and there would be a figure for materials used. He might also wish to charge a mileage rate for travel to and from the job. All this has to be worked out and totalled up. VAT at the standard rate has to be calculated on the sub-total and a final total payable arrived at. All this takes time to work out manually and then have typed up on a conventional typewriter. Even if a calculator is used, the time employed issuing just one invoice can be considerable and it is not surprising that many small businesses fall behind on their invoicing and subsequently run into trouble because they cannot get their cash in quickly enough. It is no use blaming the customer for late payment if they have yet to receive their invoice!

A simple spreadsheet set up to allow the basic figures to be inserted will do the calculations and will greatly speed the time taken to calculate and print out each invoice. A look at Exhibit 3 will reveal how this works in practice.

What to computerize

```
        VAT INVOICE
           from
        I. DRIP
        PLUMBER
                                          1 Ballcock Lane
                                          Waterlooville
                                          Hampshire
                                          SO23 3DR


                                          Waterlooville 1234

                                          VAT NO:292 2298 58


    Date/Tax Point         FEB 12 90

    Invoice Number            506.0

    To:
    S OGGY
    Leaky Hollow
    Netley by Sea
    Hampshire



    Mend 4 leaks supply  new valves

    Minimum call out fee              25.00

    Hours at £12.50          4.5      56.25

    Mileage at 25p          17.0       4.25

    Materials                         22.50



    Sub-Total                        108.00

    VAT (15%)                         16.20

    TOTAL                            124.20




    Terms: 7 days from date of invoice

    Please make cheques payable to I Drip
```

Exhibit 3

What to computerize

At the top right hand side is the trading address of the plumber together with his VAT registration number (a legal requirement on all VAT invoices). Lower down on the left hand side we have the date or tax point (this is the point at which the Customs and Excise will deem the VAT to have been charged and therefore payable, although there is now relief for small businesses from having to pay VAT which they have yet to receive from late paying customers). The address and VAT registration number are followed by the number of the invoice. VAT invoices have to be numbered sequentially. VAT officers get quite excited if when they inspect your books they find invoices missing or out of sequence and will ask awkward questions.

Next is the name and address of the customer, followed by a description of the job. The first cash item is the minimum call out charge of £25. On the next line is the hourly charge. We have set up the spreadsheet so that the figure for the number of hours (in this case four and a half) is in a box or *cell* of its own. A spreadsheet enables you to interrelate one cell with another, to take a sum in one cell and apply a formula to it in order to arrive at a new figure for another cell which is calculated and inserted automatically. The charge per hour is £12.50 and we have arranged the spreadsheet so that the cell on the same line in the cash column takes whatever figure is inserted in the hours cell and multiplies it by £12.50. In this way by inserting the figure 4.5 in the hours cell the figure of £56.25 is automatically calculated and inserted into the cash column. Materials cost £22.50 and this is simple to insert into the next cell.

Our plumber, Mr Drip, likes to charge 25 pence per mile. In this instance he travelled a total of 17 miles. By arranging for the figure for the number of miles to be inserted into its own cell we can then ask the spreadsheet to calculate the mileage charge in the cash column by multiplying the figure in the miles cell by 0.25 to arrive at a figure of £4.25.

We arrive at our sub-total by pre-programming the spreadsheet to add the figures in the cash column together and then to insert the result in the sub-total cell. To arrive at the amount of VAT payable we program the spreadsheet to take the contents of the sub-total cell, multiply the figure by 15 and divide it by 100 (15 per cent being the current standard rate of VAT). To arrive at our final figure for the total payable requires the simple calculation of adding the figure

What to computerize

in the sub-total cell to the figure in the VAT cell. Alternatively, we could arrive at the same final figure by multiplying the sub-total by 1.15.

Once this invoice has been set up it becomes known as a *boiler plate* on which subsequent invoices can be based. On the boiler plate some cells will remain the same for every invoice – the plumber's name and address, and the VAT registration number, for example. With many spreadsheet programs it is possible once you have set up your boiler plate to go through it in *automatic mode* so that as each variable item of information is inserted into the boiler plate – the invoice number, the number of hours etc. – the cursor jumps automatically to the next cell where another variable has to be inserted.

Once you have completed your invoice it is a simple matter to print out two copies. One copy is sent to the customer, the other is kept in your own files. It is of course possible to print out just one invoice to send to the customer only and save the invoice electronically on disk as your record of the transaction. However, the Customs and Excise like to approve such systems for VAT use and that can involve a visit from a VAT inspector. In any event for a small business it is much simpler in practice to have your copies of invoices held in a file on paper so you can flick through them to see which invoices are still outstanding.

Using boiler plates on a spreadsheet program can greatly improve your invoicing efficiency. In particular, if you are a one man band the time saved will be invaluable and you should find that as a result of earlier invoicing your money will come in more quickly.

Accounts

Most people in small businesses find accounts at best a necessary evil. At worst they try to shy away from doing them altogether, often with disastrous results because, like it or not, the figures are the only way of telling you how your business is doing. Unfortunately, doing the figures is tedious and often repetitive and boring work. Computers work best when they are asked to perform tedious, repetitive and boring tasks! So why not immediately bring in a computer to sort out the accounts?

There is no shortage of choice when it comes to the computer hardware itself and, more importantly, the software programs which will enable you eventually to run all your normal accountancy operations by machine. I stress the word 'eventually' because, although the computer and its software will indeed be able to perform all manner of accountancy tasks, from invoicing to working out the wages, it is quite a different matter to get it to fit in with your way of working and thinking. Eventually you will arrive at a compromise between what the system can achieve and what you want it to do. What is important is to consider whether your business is of sufficient size to justify a full blown accounting package. If you are in a service industry with fewer than fifty customers the chances are that an accounts package is not for you. As we will discuss later, the size of the business is a key factor in deciding whether to computerize the accounting operation.

Word processing

There is little doubt that, along with its ability to handle figures at high speeds, a major area where a computer can help a business is in the field of word processing. It is now possible, using the simplest word processing programs, to produce quality finished text to a consistently high standard, usually better than ordinary typewriting methods could ever have achieved. But to consider word processing as merely a substitute for the typewriter is grossly to undervalue its potential for developing any business.

Word processing offers you the facility to create tracts of words, edit them, shape the text, store and retrieve your words at will, at speeds much greater than those of conventional methods. It can be a real bonus to most businesses. The only limitation to its potential is the imagination of the people involved in using the program.

So how can a business make good use of word processing? For a start it can help with all those standard letters: reminders about overdue payments; delivery notes; covering letters for price lists, catalogues, etc. Of course, standard letters can always be printed, but they still look like standard letters. They will have to be filled in by hand and when they are, they usually look messy. With word processing, even a standard letter can be made to look exclusive to the person receiving it. This is the secret of word processing. Used correctly it can greatly enhance a company's image and bring it closer to its customers: every printed company communication can if necessary be personalized to an individual customer. It is sometimes easy in business to forget that customers are people, not simply other businesses. Word processing, used correctly, allows you to treat them like people.

So the introduction of word processing will mean greater efficiency and, above all, better presentation of company documents. It will also mean that, once trained, staff should have extra time to spend on more directly productive work. Approached in the right way, the introduction of word processing will make it easier for certain members of staff to offer much more to the business than they did when they were tied up with typewriters for much of their day.

That is not to say that the introduction of word processing means you can throw your typewriters out of the window. As we will discuss later when we come to talk about implementing your new computer system, word processing, as with all computer functions, should be introduced slowly and looked upon as an addition to rather than a replacement for existing methods. Once you are convinced that everyone is confident of using the new system, only then should you think about phasing out the old systems.

Even greater efficiency can be achieved if firms using word processing are prepared to change some of their working practices. Many companies with word processors are not getting the best value from them because of what is described as *keyboard phobia*. This irrational 'fear' of using a computer keyboard is often found to have its origin in snobbery. For years the typewriter keyboard has been seen as a symbol of office tyranny: 'Typing is women's work. Women are subservient creatures.' It is therefore unthinkable that the boss and managers, until relatively recently, usually men, should sully themselves and their status by touching their own keyboards. Far better to have someone to do it for them. The trouble is, if this prejudice is allowed to prevail the business will lose out on the benefits to be gained by having an intimate knowledge of the company's computer operation. Of course, in large businesses this is difficult to achieve and with so much sophisticated computing power available the task of understanding and developing the computer operation is naturally enough delegated to specialists.

Even so, most forward-thinking larger firms insist that their executives go on 'computer appreciation' courses so that they get a better understanding of what kinds of information they can ask the computer department to supply them with and of the complications involved in asking for various types of information. In a small business, there is unlikely to be a separate computer department and it is therefore vital that those who require the information get to grips with the way it is generated.

The computer manufacturers have long recognized keyboard phobia. Some have introduced all manner of devices to ensure that the male executive who is, of course, cut out for much better things, does not have to soil his hands by typing. Typing is certainly a skill and it takes time to learn how to do it well. But with word processing the typing process is easier to learn because eradicating errors is simpler. There is less fear of making mistakes. There is no doubt that for word processing to be really effective more people in business should be prepared to learn to type. And that starts with the boss!

Desktop publishing

In theory, desktop publishing – or DTP as it is increasingly known – has the potential to turn every business owner or manager into his own publishing centre. The idea is that it allows a manager to try out various printed corporate messages and get a real idea of what they might look like without having to commit himself to the expense and delay of involving graphic artists, typesetters and printers. For example, brochure copy can be called up on to your video screen having been written with the help of a word processing package. Using the DTP package you can then manipulate the text, change the typeface and electronically place it in the correct place on the page. Many of those functions are available on the more sophisticated word processing programs. Where DTP programs really score is in allowing you to integrate text and pictures on the same page. Some even allow you to use photographs which have been 'frame grabbed' by placing the original picture under an electronic camera. Once the frame is in the computer it can be stored away, brought back on to the VDU screen, moved into position, made larger or smaller using what is known as a 'cut and paste' operation – again, all done electronically. There are other DTP programs which offer you the facilities of more complex stand-alone graphics work stations, principally the ability to draw lines and pictures freehand and then colour them in. With all DTP systems, once you are happy with the way it all looks you can print out high quality artwork on a *laser printer* ready to send to the printer or, for small runs, use a laser printer to make multiple copies. Of course, if you opt for a colour system you will need a colour printer. This will take many businesses into areas of far higher expenditure than they might have originally envisaged. For most, the colour option will not be viable.

Desktop publishing systems can help a small business keep on top of its ever-changing print needs. For example, if you regularly place advertisements in newspapers and these ads change depending on the range of goods you have for sale, you can draw up your own advertisement in exactly the way you want it to appear in the paper. This avoids having to leave it to the newspaper's typesetters to work out and prevents errors creeping in (apart from your own!). The drawback with using DTP systems is that they are time consuming to master and there is some doubt as to whether the average small business can afford to spend the time on DTP systems when there are so many other tasks to be performed when running a business. Also, desktop publishing requires considerable computing power and that means having to opt for a more expensive microcomputer. Laser printers are not cheap either: it is essential you have one if you are to get the best from a DTP system and you are unlikely to be able to purchase one for under £1,000. It does not stop there either. The toner cartridges for the printer are expensive, costing up to £100 each. All in all you should think very carefully before embarking on desktop publishing. There are other computer applications which have a higher priority and you may find it cheaper, initially at least, to use the services of a good graphic designer and a competent printer. In addition to the work they do they will also offer valuable advice and creative input which might not necessarily be your speciality.

Databases: filing on computer

Filing is a tedious job; and finding a piece of information once filed can often be more tedious still. And filing takes up valuable office space – no one likes to see an office totally cluttered up with a welter of filing cabinets brimming over with paper. A computer can help you store much more information in a much smaller space. It can also enable you to find a relevant piece of information far more efficiently than any physical filing system, no matter how well cross-indexed that system might be.

From the time they start trading all businesses generate data – about customers, suppliers, staff and so on. Much of the business's activity can be tied up in this data and it all costs money, albeit hidden, to generate. It is very easy to look upon this data as simply a by-product of the operation; in fact, it is a valuable asset. Quite regularly you read of takeover bids where, in addition to whatever fixed assets a company might have – its factory, head office building and so on – the company doing the taking over is very keen on acquiring a new customer list or having access to a core of key staff. So these lists of customers, etc. should be valued. However, they can only be as valuable as the use you are able to make of them. What you need is a system which enables you to create your lists, analyse them, add new information, delete old information and so on.

Such a system is known as a *database*, best thought of as a very large filing cabinet. You could, for example, have every one of your customers listed in your database, together with their credit status, the amount of money they spend, details of the last transaction; even their spouse's names (useful in the preliminaries when you have to ring them to chase up a payment or try to obtain another order). The database will help you sort through your records and compile lists based on any criteria you like to establish: how many in one particular part of the country (or even the world); those who spent more than a certain amount in the last twelve months; purchasers of different product groups. Then, usually in conjunction with a suitable word processing program, you can get the computer to write personalized letters to them and print out sticky labels to speed the addressing of envelopes. The possibilities are indeed, as the glossy computer advertising says, endless.

What a database offers you is the chance of turning all your data on customers and suppliers into really useful and potentially profitable information. However, as we will discuss later, choosing a database package which will suit your needs can be difficult. Many packages, it seems, sacrifice user friendliness for sophistication and you may find that to get the best out of the more complex packages you will need to spend a lot of time getting to grips with the program. It may therefore be better to purchase a less sophisticated database package which is simpler to use.

Remember, too, that if you keep details of this sort on a computer database you are required by law to register under the Data Protection Act. This costs £56 and covers a period of up to three years at a time. Under the Data Protection Act any members of the public who think you hold records on them have the right to see those records and challenge information about them if they feel it is incorrect. You have forty days to produce the records if asked to do so by the Registrar. You are able to charge a small fee for your trouble, currently up to £10. In practice, it seems, very few people are taking up their right to view records, so thus far it is not proving to be an undue burden on business.

Stock control

Another area to consider is stock control. If you are a manufacturer a computer can help you keep track of raw materials (goods inwards or inputs) and finished goods (goods outwards or outputs). It can also link up with your sales ledger to monitor stock levels of finished goods and give early warnings when you are about to run out of your award winning, top selling line. You can even ask the computer to raise requisitions for raw materials to meet new production demands. (The ultimate is when your computer talks directly through a telephone link to your supplier's computer, and between them they work out your needs while you and your supplier spend a gentle afternoon on the golf course). Be warned, though, that such complex computer functions require highly sophisticated software to make things happen in the way you want. The more sophisticated the software, the longer it will take to integrate into your way of working, so think carefully before attempting to computerize your stock control.

Future developments: networking and training

The trend for computers to pack in more and more power seems to be showing no signs of letting up. As computers become more powerful they can run increasingly sophisticated programs. It is now common to talk about buying a 'suite' of software containing individual modules which can interrelate with each other. For example, a spreadsheet program can suddenly turn a set of figures into pie graphs and bar charts so that you can see trends more easily. As your business grows you will want to enable staff to access information from a variety of locations. In a manufacturing environment it is possible for a manager to have a direct link with the shop floor so that output can be monitored. This ability to link separate computers is called 'networking'. When considering computer applications it is wise to look ahead to the stage in your business growth where you might need to network. Remember, too, that you might need to network over some distance, using telephone lines to communicate between computers.

One of the other areas where we could see further development is in the way computers input their information. Keyboards will be around for a long time, but already computer hardware manufacturers are looking at producing cheap bolt-on hardware which will enable what is known as *Optical Character Recognition* or 'OCR'. This will mean that you will be able to take a piece of text and instead of having to key it laboriously into the computer you could instead put it through the OCR device in rather the same way as you feed a fax machine and have the text instantly displayed on your video screen. It can then be altered and stored in the same way as keyed in text. When you consider that the cost in typing time alone of inputting the amount of text held on just one floppy disk can be as much as £1,000 an affordable OCR device could provide real savings.

Another application which all businesses would do well to consider is training. We shall consider this in more detail in chapter 8, but it is worth glancing here at a few of the advances recently made in this area. Training has been much neglected in the past,

What to computerize

and small businesses in particular have found it difficult to find time for proper training initiatives within their operation. One of the reasons for this is the problem of releasing key staff to enable them to go off on courses. In small businesses their time is just too valuable to the day to day running of the operation. As a result, so-called 'open learning' courses, where learners do the work at times to fit themselves, during slack periods in the work place or at home, are becoming increasingly attractive to employers. It is in this area that microcomputers can really help.

There is now a whole range of special training programs available on floppy disk for *Computer Based Training* or CBT. These programs cover a wealth of subjects and enable the learner to work through the training material at his or her own pace. Additionally, most CBT programs allow learners to store a record of their progress to date on their own personal floppy disks. This facility allows them to pick up the course and leave it once the learning period is over. And, by linking a microcomputer with a 'videodisk player' it is possible to provide highly sophisticated one-to-one training where the learner interacts with a training package which contains not only text but also moving pictures. Interactive video disks are expensive to produce and outside the scope of small businesses, but there are a growing number being made which can be bought 'off the shelf', and the cost of the hardware is falling rapidly. Training with interactive disks can often provide a useful way in to computer literacy.

What to computerize

Key points Possible computer applications for your business

- Financial planning
  Pre-start-up
  Creating the business plan
  Assessing new product potential
- Spreadsheets
  Budgeting/cashflow forecasts
  Graphic displays/charts
  Simple invoicing
- Word processing
  Standard letters
  Forms
- Desktop publishing
  Graphics creation
- Database filing
  Creating mailing lists
  Cross-referencing suppliers
- Financial accounting
  Sales order processing
  Despatch and invoicing
  Statement production
- Production/stock control
  Purchasing
  Stock control
- Training
  Computer Based Training (CBT)
  Interactive Videodisk (IV)

4
The software

> **Outline**
>
> This chapter examines the software you may need. It includes some useful reminders of what to avoid and will help you to judge:
>
> - the type of software that will be appropriate for your business
> - how you can use it
> - what it will cost
> - which type of package you should use

Any computer system comprises two distinct parts – *hardware* and *software*. Because there is so much capital investment in the production of the equipment which makes up the hardware it is perhaps understandable that much of the marketing effort on computers and its attendant publicity is centred on shifting as many boxes of hardware as possible. However, while the hardware is of course important – without it you could not have a computer system – when it comes to business applications it is the software which really matters. And it is software which should be considered *first*, before deciding which hardware to purchase. Without good software a high performance computer is worthless. It is rather like the futility of having a Formula One racing car but not being able to afford the high octane petrol required to make it go. Having poor software would be like trying to make your high performance car perform on a tankful of diesel!

So we have to put software first in our analysis of how to choose the right systems for small business applications. Accordingly, we will consider the various hardware options in the next chapter; in this chapter we shall be looking at software and the way one sets about choosing the right software programs for specific business

41

applications. We shall also be reviewing some of the more popular software programs now available for various areas of business. This review will be by no means comprehensive but will aim to give you an understanding of the key factors involved in choosing software for your business by examining a handful of the software programs now available to the business user.

What is software?

Software is the name given to the set of instructions fed into the computer hardware which tells it how to perform the tasks required by the user. These instructions are held in computer code and are usually stored either within a silicon chip or on some kind of magnetic medium such as a floppy disk, hard disk or tape. The hardware reads the coded software instructions off the disk or tape and then puts the instructions into action in order to perform the business task required. Of course, that is an oversimplification. The hardware has to be capable of coping with all that a software program demands, but these days that is a relatively easy task for a modern, high powered microcomputer. Finding the right software in the first place is not so easy, principally because there is an apparently bewildering choice available.

What software do you need?

We keep stressing how vital it is for the computer system to operate so that it fits in with your existing business systems. However, a certain amount of compromise is usually necessary, and this is generally dependent on how logical your existing manual business systems are. We will discuss in chapter 5 how important it is to ensure that you undertake adequate planning and consultation with your staff and fellow directors in the business. This is in order to make sure you and they have a proper grasp of the business issues at stake for your operation. It is vital that you sort out those issues before you attempt to do anything else. Certainly you should avoid the temptation to rush out and buy the first likely looking software package that comes to hand. The definition of a good software package revolves around how well it can be adapted to your particular way of working. Before you can achieve that sort of match you do have to make sure you have a good understanding of the way your business operates at the moment.

It is not easy to produce one piece of catch-all software which is suitable for all business applications: the software developers have had to specialize, creating packages for much smaller markets. Some business applications require software to be written especially for them alone. This is an option you should certainly consider for your business, but such *bespoke software* as it is known can be very expensive and will take time to develop to the stage where it can be used reliably. It can also tie up a lot of effort on your part and that of your staff, as you will be required to hold the software developer's hand as he gets to grips with the requirements of your business. The bonus of bespoke software is that if it all works out as you planned, you will have a software package which is unique to your business and which could give you a competitive edge over your business rivals. Having said that, some companies which commission bespoke software programs end up selling the program to others in a similar field as a way of offsetting the software development costs. For most small businesses and especially for start-ups it is probably wiser to stick to existing off-the-peg packages or adapt or tailor such packages to your needs.

Software has come of age in recent years and there is now a good selection of well tried and tested packages on the market which, because they have already sold in substantial numbers, are available today at very reasonable prices. Some may not be what computer people describe as 'state of the art', that is, the very latest packages containing all the latest refinements. However, most new business users will not notice the subtle differences between the older versions and the new upgraded versions. There is much concerted effort on the part of the computer industry continually to pressurize the consumer into buying the latest software package available. This is for the obvious reason that they themselves are under pressure to keep up the momentum of software and hardware development. This pressure should be resisted. You want a computer operation which will work easily. The best way of ensuring this is to choose one which has served others well. There is little point in becoming a guinea pig for new, untried products. Far too much is at stake. A

The software

start-up or developing business should be able to make use of most off-the-peg software packages which have been around for years rather than months although, as we discussed earlier, some businesses do have their special needs. Whether that applies to you will depend on how unique your business and its existing operating systems are. The chances are you will be able to use an existing package or, if you need special applications, have an off-the-peg package modified to suit your needs.

Beware the complex package

Many packages these days integrate a number of functions, for example incorporating spreadsheets with graphics so you can translate columns of figures into a pictorial display. Increasingly, word processing and database software is integrated to enable you to create personalized letters for mail-shots. Most people seem to enjoy using such packages but because of their degree of sophistication it can take some time initially to get used to their way of working. The more complex a package is the more it will need to be *user friendly*, with help screens and menus to guide the user through its operation. Some of the earlier software packages might as well have been written in Chinese, so difficult were they to understand. The accompanying manual seemed to be impenetrable, with instructions so complicated users often gave up the package entirely or at best used the package only to a level way below its capabilities. When selecting software, bear this in mind. Do not choose over-complex packages or you will find that you and your staff will simply not find the time to get to grips with the way they work. A far better policy is to stick to your objectives and find a package which fulfils them, or nearly fulfils them, as simply as possible and which is truly friendly to the user – a package which enables you to achieve what you want to achieve in the shortest possible time.

Ease of use

Recently an increasing number of software packages have been released which do away almost completely with the need to follow an

The software

instruction manual. Instead, once the package is loaded into the computer it guides the user through it using a series of what are known as *on screen prompts*. Such prompts can be in the form of simple words or, increasingly, make use of *icons*: pictorial representations of functions you may wish the computer to perform for you. Thus if you wanted to save a piece of information, in other words file it away, you might point an arrow or move the cursor on the computer to a picture or icon of a filing cabinet. If you wanted to throw the information away you would point to a wastepaper basket; and so on. The use of such icon driven programs might appear a little childish and simplistic but in using computers there is no room for misplaced pride. Anything which speeds up their use and enables users to get the best out of them must be a great improvement on some of the complex instructions which used to be required. Such user friendly devices are invariably backed up by *help screens* which the user can call up if he is puzzled by some sections of the program. In some software programs you can set various on screen *help levels*. These start off by displaying all the information you need to help you through the program. Once you feel you have learnt most of the basic commands involved in operating the program you can tell the computer to display only an intermediate level of help on the screen (thus leaving more screen space for the work in progress). In some programs you can do away with on screen help altogether, so that experienced program operators can use all the screen space available. There are computer systems where you do not even have to make the decision on which level of 'help' you require: the computer automatically assesses your progress and works out how quickly you give it commands and how many times you give a false command which has to be corrected. It then sets the help level accordingly. If you slip back or are just having a bad day the help level is bumped up again. Big Brother computer is watching you!

An alternative way of getting help with the program is where you are able to draw upon *windows* of information about a particular program. These are sometimes known as *pull down menus* or *pull down windows* as they appear to be pulled down like a window blind. Such *menu-driven* programs are becoming increasingly popular and the first-time business computer user would be well advised to look for such features in any software package, as they make it far easier to get the best out of a program. There is a price to be paid in

The software

respect of the extra computer memory required to run these windows, help screens, icons and pull down menus, but computer power is relatively cheap these days and is a relatively small price to pay in return for the enhanced benefits which come from getting a new software program implemented quickly and thereby providing real benefits for the business.

If what you want to do is complex, it is even more important to look for user friendly features. As mentioned earlier, these will probably be little used once the system is installed and running but will pay huge dividends in the initial stages as you and your staff get used to the computer during the training stage of your computer initiative. The key message when selecting software programs for the first time is to be prepared to spend extra money on features which will make it as easy as possible to get the best out of the software. A survey conducted in summer 1989 discovered that the most modern electronic equipment was used to only half its capacity because of so-called 'technofear'. It would be sad if you allowed technofear to get a hold in your business because you skimped on providing the most user friendly software you could find.

Where will it lead?

When selecting software packages you do need to have an eye for the future expansion of your business. You will want to know that as you take on more business the software will be able to cope. You should seek assurances on this and where possible ask for examples of businesses similar to your own which are successfully using a given package. There is nothing more time consuming (and, indeed, costly) as having to transfer massive amounts of data to a new computer system because the software (and often hardware too) could not cope with expansion.

You may also want to consider the integration capabilities of the software with other packages. This is sometimes presented as a big selling point but its use to you is limited, as ever, to your specific computer objectives. If integration is unlikely to be a factor there is little point in paying extra for a package capable of integrating with others. One factor which is often ignored when considering the use of integrated packages is that you will be limited in how many of a package's functions you can use at any one time by the number of keyboards or work stations you have available to you in the business. Most businesses start off with just one microcomputer. If that is going to be tied up with word processing all day you will clearly need to consider having more than one machine. For example, most businesses once they are up and running can produce enough letters, reports and so on to occupy one entire work station running a word processing program all day every day. If the computer is running a word processing program which also incorporates a spreadsheet facility, database and other functions these will be wasted as that particular microcomputer will be dedicated to producing words and little else. You could therefore save yourself some money by simply having a word processing package for that particular computer.

How much will it cost?

People who write software are usually intelligent and skilled; they do not normally sell themselves cheap. So where does that leave us on the question of software prices? While it is relatively easy for the business person to quantify what his hardware costs might be – anything from £1,000 to £100,000 – software costs can only be assessed on a 'how long is a piece of string?' basis. However, the average business wanting a range of basic computing ability from spreadsheets through word processing to database filing, can often reckon on the software costing up to another 50 per cent on top of the cost of the computer hardware itself; more if any special programming is involved. So if you were planning to spend £3,000 or so on computer hardware, start expecting to count the change out of £5,000 for the complete hardware and software package! If you are looking for more sophisticated packages, such as stock control linked to invoicing and so on, it could cost you much more.

With increasing competition in the microcomputer field there are more and more off-the-peg software packages which can easily be made to fit in with your business operation. Software prices are dropping too, but not as fast in real terms as those of the hardware. With software, as with most things, it can pay to shop around. However, there are dangers in this. Most software needs *support*,

The software

that is, regular updates as new applications are found, or, as for example in the case of payroll software, changes in prevailing statutory tax rates render the software useless unless the new figures are incorporated into the package. Sometimes it might be just a matter of a *bug* being found by another user which is then eliminated and the benefit passed on to other software licence holders.

Beware pirates!

Licensing the rights to use a particular software package should be regarded as a continuing relationship between you (the user) and the software supplier. It would be unwise to jeopardize this by obtaining a copy of the software package without the proper support. Remember too that the people who produce software packages guard their expertise jealously – as well they might. After all, the only thing they have to sell is what is described as their *intellectual* property. It is unfair, immoral and illegal for their property to be copied and used by those who have not paid for the privilege of so doing. It is now well established in law that just the act of breaking the seal on a box containing a software program binds the new user to the rules of using the software as laid down in the supplier's licensing agreement. The basic price paid for the package will be for using the software on just one or two terminals. If you are using more terminals it will probably be illegal for you simply to copy as many disks as you need: you will be expected to pay for the privilege of using the software more widely. Software suppliers are not unreasonable in this, and most licensing agreements contain provisions for making back-up copies and replacing disks which get damaged or corrupted. Using software is very much a two-way street between the users and the supplier. It is wise to play fair by the rules. Needless to say, if you sink to using pirate copies of a particular software package you run the risk not only of being prosecuted for theft of copyright but also of consigning your valuable data to a system for which there will be no support if something goes wrong.

There is an additional danger which has reared its head in the last few years: that of the *computer virus*. The computer virus phenomenon appears to have originated in the United States. Mischievous and malevolent computer buffs obtain disks of proprietary software and write into it their own computer code. This code is often undetectable until it results in a catastrophe whereby all the information held on the disk is either destroyed or corrupted. This does not usually happen until the virus has transferred itself to other disks being used in the computer and thus the process replicates itself throughout an entire system causing untold damage. What perhaps started out as a jolly jape is causing terrifying nightmares for computer based businesses throughout the world. The only real way to ensure viruses do not get into your computer system is to make certain you know the origin of all the software you use and to shun any cheap disks of doubtful provenance you may be offered. It is wise, too, to make sure the computer is used only with the business software you specify. In many instances viruses have been introduced by employees running adventure games on the computer during their lunch breaks. Although not all such games contain viruses they themselves represent a potential problem if employees spend more time playing computer games than they do on the firm's real business. Such games are often very sophisticated and aimed at an 'adult' audience. Many are compulsive and get the user hooked for many, many hours. Leisure Suit Larry in the Land of the Lounge Lizards is one of the latest to sweep the US and is now going through Europe. Do not let Larry or any of his friends take over your business!

Which package?

There are said to be more than 1,000 new software packages released worldwide *every day*. Many of these are for specialist applications outside the daily operations of most business users. Others are upgrades of existing packages. Software development moves so quickly it can sometimes appear as a dazzling blur. There is no doubt that the average software developer takes real pride in enhancing his product to the nth degree. There is equally no doubt that some people in the software world often make improvements which can detract from the easy use of the package. We discussed earlier that it is the ease of use which really matters when it comes to the business user operating computers for the first time to generate more profits. Time is all-important and for this reason the newcomer to business software is, as has been said earlier, strongly advised to stick to tried and tested products. They may not be the latest, but at least you should have a better chance of establishing in advance that they work and will do the job you have in mind for your business.

The packages mentioned below form by no means a comprehensive list of what is available. They are, though, tried and tested and have been in use for some time with considerable success in many businesses. As ever, you should satisfy yourself that they will fit in with your particular business plans before adopting any of them; you might find it helpful, too, to look back at the sample applications outlined in chapters 2 and 3.

Word processing

For most businesses, particularly small ones, word processing is the most widely used type of computer program. It is important therefore that you find a package which closely matches your needs. The problem is that if you have never used a computer for producing letters and other material you will not have much of an inkling of the potential offered by word processing (WP) packages. One thing is certain: you will find that once you have one you will generate many more documents and letters than you ever did before, simply because of the new ease of doing so.

Most word processing packages boast very similar facilities. Where they vary is in the way in which they can store and retrieve documents once they have been created. This is vitally important, because you can very quickly build up a collection of several disks of documents and then find it hard to track down the letter you wrote a couple of months ago because you were restricted by the computer in the name you were able to give it. Many word processing packages allow you only a limited number of characters to describe a file. With letters, for example, you would ideally want to have the name of the addressee and the date as the filename. You would also want the computer to list the correspondence in either date order or alphabetical order of addressee. Unfortunately, many word processing programs just do not do this. Instead, they store documents in a random and haphazard fashion so you could find a letter you wrote three months ago listed next to one you wrote just a few days back.

Another useful facility when it comes to correspondence is to be able to print the address on to an envelope without having to print out the whole letter. Again, many word processing programs do not have this facility, except when you are printing out a whole list of addresses on to sticky labels.

If you are planning to produce longer documents than letters – contracts, agreements, press releases, etc. – you will also find it useful to have other features. A *search and replace* facility allows you to ask the computer to look through a document you have created and replace a word or phrase with a different one. This is useful if you have a series of standard documents where you want to alter, say, the name of the customer referred to throughout the text because, perhaps, you discover that you have misspelt his name. It is also helpful if you find you have consistently misspelt a word in a piece of text. Search and replace can also help by allowing you to use abbreviated forms when writing a piece containing the same long word or phrase. For example, while writing this chapter, instead of continually typing the phrase 'word processing' I have been able to use the abbreviation 'WP' instead. Once I have finished this section of the manuscript for the book, I shall ask the computer to go through it in search and replace mode and replace 'WP' with the words 'word processing'. Some word processing programs give you the option to change the word at every point or instead keep the abbreviation. Others give you no option and rattle through the text of the document changing the abbreviation every time. Good word processing programs give you both options.

Many people find it helpful to have a *spelling checker*. These are usually available as an extra although they are incorporated as standard into some word processing packages. There are three drawbacks with spelling checkers. First, they require considerable extra computing power if they are to be used successfully. If this power is not available they can take an inordinate amount of time to go through a document. Ideally you should have a microcomputer with a hard disk of at least 10 megabyte capacity. Secondly, even though most boast dictionaries of over 50,000 words they are often inadequate and you will find yourself having to 'top up' the dictionary with new words as you go. This will be particularly true if

The software

your business uses a lot of technical terms unique to your trading activities. The third drawback is that some spelling checker programs still use American spellings which can be particularly annoying. In choosing a spelling checker it is wise to check that a full English dictionary is available.

If you are dealing primarily with correspondence the editing facility offered to you by a word processing program will be adequate if it is keyboard based. Most word processing packages offer the facility of moving blocks of text around within a document. This facility is required relatively seldom in a letter. If, however, you are dealing with longer documents then you may wish to opt for a program which offers you the facility of using a *mouse* to edit with. The mouse will be more fully described in the next chapter on hardware; here is is just worth noting that when used in word processing it really does speed up the editing process by allowing you to mark blocks and move them very quickly. Not all word processing programs are geared to this.

Another function to consider if you are producing longer documents is *word count*. It is most useful, especially when producing copy for press releases or advertisements, to know how many words you have written as magazines and newspapers tend to measure the length of articles and the cost of insertions by the number of words.

WordStar, from MicroPro, is one of the oldest and most respected word processing programs. It tends to be keyboard based. It has good search and replace facilities and can be used with an associated spelling checker, **Spellstar**. It can also be linked to database programs and can, with its associated **MailMerge** program, be used to send out personalized letters to clients and customers. One of the big drawbacks with WordStar, however, is filenaming and listing. It is often very time consuming to retrieve an old document from a directory list because of the difficulty in tracking down the document you are looking for after it has been filed with what you considered at the time to be a most logical coded filename but which now seems gobbledegook.

Among the word processing packages which allow you to use a mouse for editing is the **GEM** package. This allows you to edit very quickly indeed, although you will of course still have to use the keyboard to do the writing itself. GEM allows you to change typefaces very quickly and, unlike older word processing programs, offers you a true WYSIWYG display. (WYSIWYG stands for 'What You See Is What You Get'.) This is most helpful if you are going to use your word processing package for laying out and designing catalogues, mailing lists, price lists and so on. For example, when you change a font style you can see the effect of the new lettering exactly as it will be printed out on the page. The one limitation to this is that you will almost certainly need to use an ink jet or laser printer as conventional dot matrix or daisywheel printers will not necessarily be able to give you the full range of printing outputs. (For more on printers see the next chapter.)

Among the newer word processing packages to come on to the market is **Manuscript** from Lotus. This is a sophisticated package offering all the basic word processing functions including multiple typefaces and the ability to integrate the package with spreadsheet packages in either numerical or graphical form. Additionally, the package gives you the basics of document design and layout. You can move whole sections of text, place them in a box which you have pre-drawn to size and then order the computer to renumber them in context for automatic indexing. The package contains a fast spelling checker containing 110,000 words (the average person's vocabulary is somewhere between 60,000 and 80,000 words). One feature which creative writers, or indeed anyone who is stuck for the right word to use in a letter, might find useful is a 15,000 word, 220,000 synonym thesaurus to help you find alternative words.

Packages such as Lotus Manuscript containing such sophisticated facilities tend to be more expensive than basic word processing programs. Manuscript costs in the region of £400; you could probably find a simpler alternative for half that amount. What you need to ask yourself is whether you really need the extra facilities being offered by the more modern packages and whether an older, tried and tested package will be easier to install and get up and running in your business.

Spreadsheets

As discussed in chapter 3, spreadsheets are a must for any start-up or growing business. They will help you in the planning stages as

The software

you try to work out the effect of spending money on various parts of your proposed business and forecast the net profit (or loss) there will be on your various activities. Once the business is up and going a spreadsheet package will help you analyse how well you are doing and help you measure performance against budget on a month by month basis. Many of the more modern spreadsheet packages tend to be aimed at the executive in a large corporation who is faced with the weekly task of having to make a presentation to his bosses and colleagues about how well various projects are going. For this reason the emphasis these days is for the software developers to produce spreadsheet packages which are geared to presenting figures in graphical form. You have to be clear about whether this is a facility you will really need in your small business. After all, at the end of the day the figures are the figures. What matters is that you understand their significance. If you do and you can get all the information you need from looking at the bottom line of a conventional cash flow document then do not bother with a graphics representation of your spreadsheet package. If you prefer looking at a picture rather than masses of figures, then the modern spreadsheet package is for you.

One of the most basic spreadsheet packages which has been around for several years is **CalcStar** from MicroPro. This is the brother package to WordStar and is very simple to get to know and use. Much is made of the number of cells which are available, that is, individual areas into which you can put information to be related by command to other cells within the spreadsheet. Modern spreadsheet packages often boast huge numbers of cells. With CalcStar you can have as many as 5,000 cells, or more normally around 1,500. Most small businesses would simply not require such large spreadsheets. Indeed, it is often confusing to have so much information on one sheet, as it is only possible to view or *window* a very small number of cells on your visual display unit at one time. In practice it is far better to break a large spreadsheet down into smaller spreadsheets. A fully integrated spreadsheet is all very well but it is very easy to make a catastrophic mistake in just one of the formulae and end up with the almost impossible job of trying to track it down. So do not be persuaded by promises of large numbers of cells. You probably will not need them.

A tried and tested program such as CalcStar gives you all the basic facilities you require in a spreadsheet package. You will be able to set up cash flows covering sales and expenditure, allowing you to keep a running total of cash flow into and out of your business which should tally with the state of your current account balance at the bank. Also, all spreadsheet packages such as CalcStar should allow you to project forward so that you can see the effects of continuing the current trends in sales and expenditure. In this way you will be able to see when you are going to break even and then go into profit – or indeed, when you will finally exceed your overdraft limit. Either way you will want to make the best use of the information offered to you by the spreadsheet package so that you can plan accordingly.

CalcStar will help you with estimating and with preparing invoices and statements. Using *regression* and *projection* functions you can calculate how well matters are going and how matters might turn out in the months to come. CalcStar is a simple program to operate and contains more than enough facilities for the average small business user.

One of the most popular microcomputer spreadsheet packages in recent years has been **Lotus 1-2-3**, which owed much of its success to its popularity on IBM micros. This is a very powerful spreadsheet package; and besides containing all the usual spreadsheet package facilities, it really scores in its speed of recalculation, which is extremely fast. But again, a small business using the spreadsheet package just a few times a month is unlikely to be troubled by a spreadsheet program which has a relatively slow recalculation time. The only situation in which this does become a drawback is where the spreadsheet package is being used constantly to assess and analyse endless figures.

SuperCalc is another well known, tried and tested package. There is a modern version called **SuperCalc 5** which reads and writes Lotus 1-2-3 files and enables you to create high quality colour graphics with a 3D effect. It also has a facility seldom found on older spreadsheet packages, namely the ability to track down 'bugs' in the spreadsheet: that is, cells which contain erroneous formulae which will be causing all sorts of false calculations to be made. SuperCalc 5 has powerful debugging and auditing systems which lets you see just how each cell is formulated and then checks for bugs by tracing all cells which feed into that formula. SuperCalc5 has high quality

The software

fonts, rules and shadings and is aimed again at the large corporation executive market which will have access to colour visual display units and high quality colour printers which can turn out professional looking reports. Yet again, if you are a small business, nice though it would be to have such a facility, can you really justify such extra expenditure?

Another new alternative spreadsheet package is Microsoft's **Excel**. This claims to be the only spreadsheet package specifically created for the production of graphics. It has a true WYSIWYG display and like SuperCalc 5 can read and write Lotus 1-2-3 files. You can also use a mouse to move about the program. Excel will produce bar charts, line graphs and pie charts and in colour if you so wish. However, once again you will need extra, more expensive, hardware if you are to take full advantage of this spreadsheet package.

As with other software, with spreadsheet packages it is important to obtain the solution which is right for your business application at a price a business can afford. There is all too frequently a bewildering choice. Do not allow yourself to be persuaded to buy more than you really need. The more sophisticated a package is, the harder it will be for you to get the best out of it, particularly in the initial stage of implementing the program.

Databases

The big problem with databases, more acute it seems, than with any other kind of software, is the way in which the software developers appear to have rushed ahead with ever more powerful packages leaving the poor user with great difficulty in making any sense out of the software he is being offered. Databases originally came from the mainframe end of the computer world where the ability to handle enormous quantities of data with great speed was very much the name of the game. Moreover, the speed requirement was coupled with a need to be able to relate each piece of information to any other within the database. This pressure to sort large amounts of information tended to colour the judgement of the software developers when it came to devising suitable database packages for the business user. What the small business primarily needs is a simple system of filing the names and addresses of its customers and suppliers in order to be able to use the lists to create mail-shots to establish new sales leads, chase up outstanding invoices, and so on. The range of uses to which a database can be put is limited only by the imagination of those using them. However, for a small business you want a limited number of applications which you can easily put into practice. For this reason you must find a program which is user friendly.

Among the most user friendly systems I have used is **DataEase** from Sapphire. It is classically designed to be very quickly picked up by the small business user who has little experience of computers. With this program you can be creating files of your customers or suppliers within a few minutes of starting the tutorial disk. This disk, coupled with the manual, shows you how to get the best out of the software. After a day or so of use you should be able to run your first report whereby you search through a list of files looking for different criteria. For example, you might wish to produce a list of customers who have spent more than a certain sum with you in the last six months; or one of customers who have spent nothing with you in the last year. You might use this latter list for a specially designed mail-shot to find out why they have not been in touch to place an order. Alternatively, you might simply want to cross them off your mailing list and concentrate on those who do spend with you on a regular basis. Like most other database packages, DataEase is a fully relational database which means that you can search files and sort through them on any basis you choose. Where this database program scores is that you are given clear instructions on how to set up various pre-determined on screen forms to enable you to do this. In addition, the program allows you to modify these forms at a later stage as circumstances and requirements change without corrupting the information you have already fed into the computer.

The developers of DataEase claim that you can use the software to generate forms, letters, mailing labels, invoices, purchase orders, customer's forms and so on. Indeed, they say you can automate virtually every part of your business administration activities. That is quite a tall order, but DataEase is certainly a good starting point for a small business contemplating using a database for the first time.

Among the best known of the database packages is the Ashton

The software

Tate **dBase** range. In use now are **dBaseII, dBaseIII** and **dBase IV**, plus a number of variations on these, each of these versions being an improvement on the previous one. The trouble with the dBase range is that, as with so many other database programs, they are highly complicated for the tyro computer user to get to grips with. On the plus side, the database programs themselves are very powerful and the programs are able to handle large amounts of data and sort through it very quickly indeed. However, that power is traded off against user friendliness. The problem seems to be that if you want a database to be really flexible you end up with the user being almost cast adrift, confronted with so many options in the way the database program can be implemented that he ends up taking none of them. This scenario is not helped by manuals which often appear impenetrable to the casual business user. Even when they try to be user friendly they often miss the mark. Take this little section from the dBaseII manual.

String operators generate string results.
 + = string concatenation (exact)
 − = string concatenation (moves blanks)
Concatenation is just another one of those fancy computer buzzwords. All it really means is that one character string is stuck onto the end of another one . . .

Well, that should be clear enough!

People in the computer business often rave about the power of database programs. This power is useless to you as a business user unless you can make use of it efficiently. Powerful database programs really do need experts to set them up and maintain them. That means that every time you want to change the way your database operates you will be involved in more cost. For the average small business user a simple database program will more than suit requirements for a year or two at least.

One other software tool you might like to consider is one of the growing number of programs which attempt to help you order your thoughts. Many of these spring from database software but they are generally much more user friendly, allowing you to enter information into a computer in a random way and then sort it out so that your unstructured ramblings come together and help you form some coherent thoughts on a given subject. One such program which seems to be gaining ground is **Agenda** from Lotus. It is billed in its advertising as a 'thought processor'. The idea is that using your Agenda program you enter bits of information randomly in the same way as you would write them on a note pad. These are classed as 'items'. You then 'categorize' the items in any way you choose: as names, dates, places, products, areas and so on. The program enables you to recategorize as often as you like.

For the small business person a program such as Agenda can be a great help in processing contact names and addresses, classifying them into various categories and having them at your fingertips when the need arises. It will also help if you are developing ideas for new products. It has to be said, however, that such software is perhaps best for those who already have a liking for and a facility with computers; and that the use of such 'thought processing' software may not (initially at least) result in immediate profit for your operation.

The overall message when trying to select suitable database software is: *do not* opt for a program so powerful that it cannot be used easily and put to work quickly in your business. Go for one which is clearly user friendly and limits your options by giving you clear guidance. In this way you will not be overwhelmed by the sheer complexity of what a database can do for you. In business there are certain common needs which can normally be fulfilled by most database programs. The secret is to ensure that you find a program which helps you get it into operation in the shortest possible time and then allows you to build on what you have started with.

Finding your files

While we are on the subject of databases we might mention the whole question of searching for files stored on disk over a period of time. It is advisable for new users of computers in business to consider in advance one of the very real problems which face most computer users after a year or two. It is very easy to accumulate hundreds of files on numerous disks. These could be letters and documents created using word processing programs, various spreadsheets or, indeed, database files. We discussed earlier how many software programs do not really allow you to name these files in a manner that

The software

remains sensible when viewed months later. This makes it very difficult to unclutter your disks and weed them of out of date or unwanted information. Many people tend to allow their stack of disks to get ever taller, with the result that when you come to look for one vital piece of information it is submerged in a welter of extraneous data. As we have discussed, updating your disks and clearing out unwanted files is time consuming; disks are relatively cheap and you never know when you might need the information. However, it is a different matter if your computer uses a hard disk. These can range in capacity from anything from the equivalent of ten floppy disks to fifty and thus represent huge amounts of memory. Yet despite their capacity, even hard disks can get full very quickly and then you are faced with the choice of not using the hard disk or doing something about clearing out the dead wood files.

Fortunately, there are growing numbers of software programs which do allow you to view the contents of files quickly and thus speed up an otherwise laborious process. One such program is **Magellan**, again from Lotus. Aptly named after the great explorer, Magellan attempts to take you on 'a journey of discovery through your files'. How it works in practice is this. Normally to view your saved files you would have to call up each file individually from its directory. Particularly where long documents are involved this can take a considerable time for each file. Using Magellan you simply highlight the file you wish to view in the directory and the contents are displayed instantly. Using such a program it is a relatively simple matter to speed through the disks, delete files you do not need and free up valuable working and storage space on the disk.

Accounts

For a small business an accounts package which incorporates the range of formal entry systems required to meet with modern accountancy practice needs careful consideration. The first step should be to discuss the possibility of computerizing your accounts with your accountants. They may have a system which is already in use and tried and tested with them. They may have other clients who could tell you their experiences with a particular accountancy software package. Above all you have to remember that an accounts package will not necessarily bring you more profit, especially in the

The software

early stages of the business. You simply will not have enough throughput of business to justify the computerization of this area. Where accounts packages really score is if they enable you to free up valuable staff time spent on 'doing the books'. However, it may be that certain areas are time consuming while others are not. For example, if you are in the catering business employing a number of people on a casual, part-time basis, you will in most cases be expected by the Inland Revenue to deduct PAYE and National Insurance contributions from their wages. It can be tedious and time consuming to do this manually, especially where large numbers of employees are involved, all with differing tax codes and all working differing numbers of hours. A computerized payroll operation could help in this area. It would be wrong, though, to go for a full blown accounts package on computer just to sort out a payroll problem. What is required is the ability to implement an accounts package on a modular basis. You can then 'grow' the accounts computerization with your business.

There are a number of modular accounts packages on the market; among those which have been well tried and tested over the years is **Pegasus**. Pegasus has been around for a long time and although relatively expensive if you buy all the modules at once it does give you a fully integrated operation which should result in savings when it comes to auditing your books. Many accountants are familiar with Pegasus but again you must check to ensure your advisers will be happy to work with the program.

Installing an accounts package should really be regarded as a second stage in the computerization of your business. There are other more pressing areas to be considered first and certainly areas which will result more quickly in better profitability.

The software

> **Key points** Choosing software
>
> - Set priorities for computerization
> - Go for simplicity
> - User friendliness is paramount
> - Opt for tried and tested programs
> - Seek out existing users for software endorsement
> - Make sure there is ongoing support for the software
> - Beware pirate software
> - Have an eye for future compatibility

5
The Hardware

> **Outline**
>
> This chapter will help you to choose the best hardware for your business and we explain:
>
> - what you need to know about hardware before you start to make a decision
> - how to understand computer jargon
> - which hardware will be best for your business
> - how to choose monitors and printers
> - buying second hand

In the last chapter we established that the most important part of any computer installation is the software. By deciding what software you need to meet your business needs you can be more certain of getting the best computer solution to fit those needs. Virtually all hardware will run most software. Having said that, there are great differences between the types of hardware available. In this chapter we will assess some of these and will look at the key questions you should be asking, both of the equipment in relation to yourself and of the people trying to sell it to you. We will also review some of the current makes of hardware available and while this review will not be comprehensive it will serve to help you assess what combination of hardware will be most suited to your business needs.

What you need to know about hardware

Before we go any further let us have a few definitions. Hardware is the name given to all the 'hard' bits of the computer system: the processor unit, the keyboard, the screen, the printer and so on – the

The hardware

bits you can actually reach out and touch. When people first start to discuss computers, it tends to be the hardware which is mentioned first. This tendency towards concentrating all discussion on the hardware is perhaps understandable. After all, the hardware is there for everyone to see. Not only that, the history of the computer business has been dominated by the big companies which have made substantial investment in tooling and production. This level of investment gives continuing impetus to the need to maintain a constant stream of new buyers for the thousands of computers being turned out every week worldwide. Little wonder, then, that the production effort is backed by such a powerful marketing thrust. However, despite what the advertisements say, do remember that, particularly in business applications, it is software which really counts, time and time again.

Capacity and speed

Choosing the right hardware revolves around two key factors. First, there is the question of *capacity*, or *memory* as it is often known; and secondly, there is *speed*. Speed is not usually a factor when it comes to small businesses in the initial stages of start-up, particularly if the computer is only going to be used from time to time. However, as we will discuss later it can be crucial if your day to day operation is likely to depend on a high level of computer usage.

The more powerful a software program is, the more capacity your computer will need to run it. Similarly, if you are planning to store a large amount of data in the form of, for example, names and addresses of customers and suppliers you will need capacity for that too. It goes without saying that the more capacity you specify the higher the cost of the computer hardware, although these days adding extra memory to a computer system is a relatively cheap option and you should not shrink from paying for extra capacity if you think you are going to need it. Alternatively, you could opt for a system which allows you to 'bolt on' additional memory as it is required. Either way, it is foolish to skimp on capacity. There is nothing more frustrating than working with a computer system so overloaded with data in relation to its capacity that it simply cannot handle straightforward requests for analyses or refuses to save new or existing files you have been working on because its memory cannot cope. In short, if you think you will have a demand for high capacity and money is not an overriding factor, make sure you buy a system with a hard disk (see under 'Memory' below) and make sure that hard disk has the biggest capacity available. Even if you do not make use of it at first you will come to bless your decision later on as your business grows and the computer system becomes fully integrated with your commercial operation.

As mentioned earlier, when choosing hardware it will also be necessary to consider the speed of the computer. Not all computers operate at the same speed, and some, for complex operations, can be painfully slow. You need to ensure that if you are looking for fast service from your machine you get one which can operate quickly. Unfortunately this is not as straightforward as it sounds. Unlike memory or capacity there is no easy way of measuring the operating speed of a computer system in terms of how quickly the machine will perform the tasks you set it. You will hear talk of 16 bit and 32 bit machines. The higher the number of 'bits', the faster the machine will operate. However, much of the final speed of function performance depends on the *operating system* used by the hardware, the nature of the software programs you use to run on the machine and how much stored information it has to sort through. Until relatively recently the operating systems for most small computers seemed to be standardizing on what is known as MS-DOS. In 1989, however, IBM, who although relative newcomers to the microcomputer market now dominate sales of PCs, brought out a new operating system called OS2. OS2 is being promoted as a much superior system to MS-DOS and naturally enough IBM are doing all they can to promote it. As yet there is still relatively little real experience of the system in business use to make a proper judgement. Speed is a function of memory, too. A machine which is struggling with too little memory can appear to be very slow indeed. So once again it will pay you to opt for a system which has the largest capacity memory you can afford. However, when it comes to issues of speed overall it is best not to get bogged down in the jargon associated with the speed of the hardware. The best way forward is to look at what other businesses are using and ask them whether the combination of hardware and software works fast enough for their needs, bearing in mind that their needs may not be the same as yours.

The hardware

Colour or monochrome?

There are other issues to address when deciding on hardware: for example, whether to have colour or monochrome monitors. Some would consider colour a luxury; others see it as a necessity. Certainly it is arguable that for basic word processing functions where you will simply be producing ordinary letters which would normally be typed on a conventional typewriter a colour screen will not really add to the operation. However, if you are into desktop publishing and would be looking to produce page layouts in colour, clearly a colour screen is going to be vital. And then you will find that the factors which affect the choice of a colour screen will affect other elements of the hardware, such as printers.

In this chapter we will consider some of the options and how you might set about choosing the right hardware to go with the software solution you have decided is best for your business.

Beyond the jargon

This section could be headed 'bits, bytes and bugs'. These are just a sample of the buzzwords used by people in the computer industry. Like all jargon, used properly, these words serve as a useful shorthand in discussions of computer systems; but to outsiders they can often make a difficult subject impenetrable. There is something to be said for the business person avoiding being sucked into the computer world and its concomitant jargon, but inevitably some words do come in useful. A few definitions, then.

Memory

As outlined above, this can best be described as the amount of 'thinking' and storage space a computer has. Broadly speaking there are two types of memory. ROM stands for *Read Only Memory*. These are computer instructions held on silicon chips within the computer. The computer can have access to this information but the information cannot be changed – or 'written to', as they say in the computer world. Usually ROM chips hold basic operating instructions which enable the computer system to start up.

The hardware

RAM stands for *Random Access Memory*. Again, this is information held on silicon chips, but this type can be accessed by the computer, altered, added to or deleted from. The amount of memory contained in either ROM or RAM is measured in *bytes* – best understood as the space required to store one character, i.e. a letter or digit. (You will often hear computer people refer to *bits*. This is the basic building block of writing computer software programs but really speaking it is of little use as a term to the business user. Neither is the term *nibble* (four bits) except for its amusement value! The term which matters is the byte and its various multiples.) A thousand bytes is known as a *kilobyte* and you will hear computer capacity referred to in kilobytes and, in some cases, *megabytes* (millions of bytes).

The same terms of capacity are used when it comes to *floppy disks* or *diskettes* which provide another way of storing information to be accessed and changed at will. Floppy disks, or 'floppies' as they are often known, are thin plastic disks which are coated with magnetic material, similar to that on an audio cassette tape. Such disks are capable of having large amounts of computer data recorded on to them. The most popular sizes are three and a half inch and five and a quarter inch diameter disks. There are a number of versions of floppy disk – you will hear terms such as *double sided, double density, 96 tracks per inch tpi*. Each computer requires the correct disks as specified by the manufacturer. Before they can be used the disks need to be *formatted*. This is a process of running the disks in your computer with a special formatting program which is usually included within the disk operating system. Disks vary in capacity but usually have space in the order of 512 kilobytes – enough to store around 25,000 words of text.

The advantage of floppy disks is that they can be removed from the computer and transferred to another machine; they can even (in suitable protective packaging) be sent through the post. The disadvantage of floppies is that despite their large capacity it is very easy to accumulate large quantitites of disks full of data and it can be inconvenient to keep having to change the disks in the machine. To counter this problem many microcomputer systems offer *hard disks*, sometimes also known as *Winchester* disks. These are rigid disks fixed within the computer which cannot be physically removed. Their advantage is their vast capacity – anything from 10 megabytes upwards. It is now quite possible for all software programs used in a

The hardware

business to be stored on the hard disk, making it much easier to switch between them when required and freeing the floppy disks for information which is regularly updated or perhaps needs to be transferred physically. External hard disks are also available to upgrade older machines with no internal hard disks or augment existing storage systems. A very recent development is the *Winchester Cassette*, which enables the magnetic storage medium to be extracted from the hard disk drive and transported just like a floppy.

Peripherals

A *peripheral* is the name given to anything which is tied into the computer system other than the computer itself, which you will sometimes hear referred to as the *Central Processing Unit* or CPU. The screen on which you view computer entries – the *Visual Display Unit* or VDU – is a peripheral. You will also hear it referred to as a *monitor* or *screen*. Here you usually have a straight choice between monochrome (either green, yellow/orange or black and white) or colour. Colour screens, whilst they sound a luxury, can often help when it comes to using spreadsheets and are particularly effective if you are planning to display your information in graphic form.

Printers are another kind of peripheral. You will hear of *dot matrix* printers which are the least expensive type of printer, capable of producing very fast printouts. However, the quality can often be poor, as the process relies on around twenty tiny pins to transfer the letters either on to heat- or pressure-sensitive paper or ordinary paper via a conventional inked ribbon. Some dot matrix printers offer *Near Letter Quality* or NLQ where each letter is struck twice, giving a bolder image. However, to do this the speed of printing is slowed down and thus it takes about twice as long to print out each document.

True letter quality printing is achieved using either a *daisywheel*, where each individual character is held on a plastic wheel which is then struck through a ribbon in the same way as a conventional electric typewriter, or one of the more modern alternatives now replacing daisywheel printers, namely *laser* or *ink jet* printers. The former is capable of producing large quantities of high speed, high quality printing using laser and photocopier technology to transfer the image to the printer. The ink jet printer uses a technology not dissimilar to that used in the dot matrix but to achieve high quality results; however it cannot produce large quantities of printed material at such high speeds as the laser printer.

If you want to get one computer to talk to another you will need facilities to *network*. At its simplest, networking takes the form of linking the computers up by cable. However, you will probably need special networking software to make it happen and you may need special cables. There is now available a range of so called *smart cables*. These cables have special connectors on each end which contain silicon chips capable of deciphering the way different computers send out their messages. Thus it is possible to get computers of different make and design to talk to each other. If you wish to have your computers communicate over long distances you will need to purchase a suitable *modem*. A modem is a piece of equipment which enables computer information to be sent to another computer down a telephone line. Another piece of kit you might wish to consider is an *uninterruptible power supply*. This device is fitted between the power socket and computer and ensures that in the event of a power failure a current is maintained for long enough for you to save the work currently in hand. An uninterruptible power supply will also guard against momentary blips in the power supply which can wreak havoc with a computer program. It is particularly useful if you are working in rural areas where the power supply can be subject to frequent fluctuation and failure.

The amount of jargon is almost endless in the computer world. You will hear salesmen talk of *firmware* which, as it name implies, is a kind of cross between hardware and software which enables a program to be stored on a chip within a computer. This chip can be removed and replaced by another with different programming. You may also hear talk of *dongles* – devices which protect software from being pirated or used without authorization. A similar device involves the use of a *smart card* or *smart reader*. These devices are used when a piece of software is licensed for limited periods of time or in some cases for a limited number of uses. For example, you may be using a piece of software which needs constant updating. One such is **Factotum**, a data management program which is licensed on a time basis and comes with what the suppliers describe as a *guard card*. This card is validated by the suppliers and has an expiry date

The hardware

on it. The computer checks the date against the card in relation to the date on its own internal clock. Once the date has passed the computer will deny access to the software. A new card covering a further licensing period has to be paid for before the software can be used. Increasingly, so-called *smart cards* are being used – these are credit card like pieces of plastic which contain a silicon chip. This chip can be programmed by the software supplier and reprogrammed by returning the card to them. Sometimes such safeguards are built in to the disk itself. You will often find that software suppliers will release a program in a demonstration form; for example, a database program might enable you to try out the way it works but limit you as to the number of records you can file away. In this way you can try the software to see if you like it but you cannot cheat and put it into practical use without paying the correct licence fee for the full software. Such devices are sometimes programmed into the disk itself. Whatever safeguards are used on a piece of software you must ensure you do not fall foul of them by using a pirated or illicitly copied program. If you do, you will be storing up trouble for yourself. There is nothing worse than finding out that you have incomplete or substandard software months after you have started using it and having stored thousands of records using the system. The cost of losing this data will far outweigh the savings you made by buying the software 'off the back of a lorry'. Not only that: if you get caught, for example by calling in a computer engineer who reports the illicit software or because a disgruntled employee informs on you, you could find yourself facing a substantial fine and damages if prosecuted for breach of copyright.

Compatibility

One thing which is vital to check is compatibility. If you are just getting into computers this will not on the face of it appear to be a problem. Obviously if you have existing computer equipment you will want to make sure that if at all possible new equipment will be capable of running your existing software programs and handling the mass of data you already hold on disk. However, even if you are a first time buyer it is important to look to the future to ensure you are not buying a system that is already becoming obsolete.

The hardware

One key area is to look at the *operating system*. This is the term used for the piece of software which in essence tells the computer how to 'think'. It is often held internally on ROM chips although in some cases it is held on the hard disk or has to be loaded from floppy disk. The majority of micros, as we saw earlier, now use an operating system known as MS-DOS and it is probably wise to opt for equipment with this type of operating system. However, there are two other operating systems which are gaining ground. The first is UNIX, an operating system that was heralded years ago as the shape of things to come. Unfortunately, Unix has been a long time coming and really only comes into its own on larger computer installations. There is some doubt about how much use it will be to the small business person using a microcomputer. The more serious threat to compatibility is the new OS2 operating system from IBM. A new breed of microcomputer is being launched on the back of OS2, aimed primarily at the executive market. Unfortunately, the new computers and their associated software have little track record yet in the world of business. To be safe you will probably be better off sticking to MS-DOS systems with tried and tested software.

IBM have a dominance in the microcomputer market. Figures vary as to just how great that dominance is; some say they have anything up to 75 per cent of the market. What this means is that if you decide to opt for a non-IBM machine you will be faced with another compatibility issue: the ability of your hardware to cope with software written to run on IBM machines. You will hear the term *IBM compatible* a lot. However all compatibility is not the same and you will have to check the level and ease of compatibility. For example, most modern micros claim to be able to read IBM disks. However, with some of them you have to type in so many commands to get them to do so that it makes it impractical in a commercial environment to rely on such programs. The answer is to check and check again and do not take the salesman's say-so as gospel.

The important thing is to ensure that you use and allow to be used only those bits of jargon you understand. Anything else should be spelled out so you can see if it is something which fits in with your ideas about what you need for your business.

Hardware – top of the pops

At the top of any list of microcomputer manufacturers will come the name **IBM**. There is an old saying in the computer industry, 'Nobody got fired for buying IBM' which reflects the fact that historically most people selecting a microcomputer for their business have, when in doubt, tended to play safe and purchase a machine which really does have a household name. What many people forget, however, is that IBM were relative latecomers to the microcomputer game. Initially such firms as Atari and Commodore were very much at the forefront of supplying small business computers, with the powers that be in IBM rather disdaining what they then regarded as the rather small and unprofitable end of the computer market, preferring to concentrate on the larger mini and mainframe systems – a market which they dominated. However, once top IBM executives realized the potential of the microcomputer market there was no stopping them. Within a couple of years the technological skills of 'Big Blue' (the nickname comes from IBM's corporate colours) were combined with its manufacturing might and marketing muscle to unleash a world beating range of microcomputers. It was IBM which was responsible for championing the MS-DOS operating system and ousting the CP/M operating system which up to that time had been heavily promoted as an industry standard in the computer world.

Today IBM manufactures a wide range of microcomputers. All of them will run virtually all of the business software you are ever likely to need, subject to constraints of usable memory. IBM micros come with varying degrees of memory and speed and they are constantly being upgraded. You also know that they have their reputation to maintain and that means good product knowledge among the people who sell and good support once you have bought your micro. Indeed, would-be traders in IBM machines have to qualify by going through a course of comprehensive training before they are allowed to become stockists of IBM PCs. There is no doubt you will get unparalleled service when you buy IBM. So if the machines are so good, the product knowledge of the people selling them so great, the after sales support so wonderful and the capability to run virtually any business software on the market so comprehensive, why bother to look any further?

The answer to that question lies in the fact that because of IBM's dominance in the market place other manufacturers of computer hardware try even harder to give the customer that little bit extra. They try harder in two ways. First, on price – for what they are, IBM machines tend to be more expensive. Secondly, on features – most of the machines produced by IBM's competitors have many more features, often of the so called 'state of the art' variety which cynics would say means that they probably have not stood the test of constant use in a business environment. We discussed earlier that it is best to take a conservative view of such features and opt only for those which have been around for some time to ensure you do not get sucked into using something which does not really work under pressure and which, rather than provide business solutions, could give you real problems in the future.

When it comes to price, however, it is a different matter. It is possible to make real savings by shopping around; but you do have to be sure that you are not sacrificing other key factors such as support and compatibility in the process. You may also find yourself having to use software packages which are less well known, which will mean that it will be less easy to ask other users how well the system works simply because there are likely to be fewer people using that system.

This is not to say, however, that other hardware is not up to the mark. For example, there is a range of so called *IBM clones* available. These are produced by a variety of different manufacturers and they are to all intents and purposes exactly the same as, or very similar to, the IBM range of microcomputers. However, because they do not carry the famous badge and all the support and back-up which goes with it, they can be substantially cheaper. True IBM clones should be capable of running all software originally intended for IBM machines, and you ought to have little trouble using such clones to help you with business applications. Indeed, many large-scale users of microcomputers, such as accountancy firms, have tended to opt for IBM clones rather than the original and genuine article.

As you might imagine, IBM have been none too happy about

The hardware

other manufacturers using what are essentially the fruits of their technological research and marketing strategy as a base for producing machines which can undercut IBM hardware. It is said that this was one of the factors which influenced IBM's decision to produce a new range of machines which run on the new OS2 operating system superseding MS-DOS. IBM have dubbed these new computers 'PS2' and they have been launched with a heavy marketing effort. As a result of this marketing effort and IBM's ability to dominate the market, IBM seem to have gained themselves a real edge over the competition which has been left floundering. The question for new users of PCs is whether to opt for the new IBM machines or stick with the older ones. Certainly the new machines look like being at a premium price for some time. Certainly they have yet to boast much of a track record in a business environment; but you may feel you can overlook that shortcoming as they have the IBM reputation to back them up in the relatively unlikely event of something going wrong. In the final analysis, the decision on what hardware to purchase may well revolve around price. If, however, you feel computers will really dominate your business you should seriously think about starting in the way you mean to go on, and if PS2 and its operating system OS2 are going to get a foothold – as seems likely – as long as you can afford the extra cost involved, this could well be the route for you to pursue.

Assuming you are looking for straightforward business applications which have been tried and tested and that you feel that computer usage is not going to become dominant in your business, what then are the other makes of hardware to be considered? There are scores of manufacturers other than IBM and it would be impossible to give an analysis of all of them. None the less, there is a handful of names which should appear on your shortlist of potential hardware suppliers.

One to consider seriously is **Compaq**. They, like other manufacturers of hardware, are keen to exploit the latest advances in chip technology. Compaq have certainly been front runners in doing this. The new silicon chips allow machines to process information faster, thus satisfying the never ceasing quest for more power in a microcomputer. When you first start using a micro such power seems awesome but as your knowledge and facility with the machine grows you will find you too will require more power from the machine. Compaq have a good range of microcomputers with varying capacities based on the Intel 386 chip. The most powerful is the Compaq Deskpro 386/25 which has hard disk, plus slots for five and a quarter and three and a half inch floppy disks. It also offers a wide selection of options for computer based graphics, but as we have discussed before, that kind of facility may be superfluous for day to day business use. There are less expensive machines in the Compaq 386 range, including the Portable 386. Compaq were among the leaders in the production of portable PCs. Portability can be important if you are a small businessperson wanting to have computing power both at home and in your work place. It is also useful if you need to have computing power at your elbow when you visit customers, either as a sales aid or to help you fulfil an order. Insurance salesmen, for example, increasingly use them to work out projected returns on policies. Tradesmen can use them to help estimate materials required to complete a given job. A portable PC gives you the facility always to have a powerful aid on hand. Some of the earlier so-called 'portables' were so heavy that you would have needed an all-in wrestler to help you carry them about! These days the trend is for smaller, truly portable computers which, while they might have limited memory, have the ability to be able to transfer or *dump* information from the portable to your free standing microcomputer in the office. Probably a better solution than starting with a portable is to have a non-portable micro and if you need portability buy one of these smaller and relatively cheap portables later.

Another range of microcomputers you may wish to consider is that produced by **Tandy**. Their 4000 LX series is the latest set of computers based on the Intel 80386 chip. Once again, they stress the graphics capability of the machines and their capacity to handle mathematics–intensive applications such as spreadsheets.

If you *are* planning to use graphics, and in particular if you are aiming to go in for desktop publishing, there is one range of computers which has to be on your list for consideration. This is the **Macintosh** range produced by the Apple Corporation. The Apple Corporation have been at the forefront of producing highly user friendly systems which incorporate a software specially written for Apple hardware making considerable use of icons. These icons make it very easy to get to grips with the software and productive use can be had from the system at a relatively early stage of training.

The hardware

Invariably, Apple Macintosh computers make consiserable use of a mouse to control its various functions. This is a great asset when carrying out graphic based tasks and editing on a word processing program. It is arguable how much use it is when using number based software such as spreadsheets and accounting packages. However, if you want a stylish all-purpose machine which is user friendly the Macintosh range is worth close consideration.

Among the features of the Macintosh range of computers is the small amount of physical space they take up on a desk. This is often referred to as the *footprint*. The smaller the footprint, the less space is taken up by the computer. Obviously, this can be an important factor if you are using a normal sized desk and you need to have room to carry out other day to day office functions. The alternative is to give the computer a desk all to itself, but in small businesses office space is at a premium and you simply may not have the room. Apple have made this reduced footprint issue into almost an art form. Among their latest machines is the Mac IIcx which has a footprint of just 12 by 15 inches. Additionally, in recognition of the coming difficulties and potential dominance of the IBM inspired OS2 operating system, the machine has the capability of reading and writing not only to MS-DOS but to OS2 as well.

Another range of hardware which boasts a small footprint comes from **Apricot**. They have consistently produced stylish computers which look at home in any office environment. In the past the overall physical screen size has tended to be rather small, and indeed, their almost dainty approach to computer hardware design has meant the original Apricot range seemed to attract only female users, especially as the company favoured cream as the predominant colour for the computer casings. It is said that a few years back when they were looking to expand sales to thrusting male executives some bright individual in Apricot hit on the idea of offering an alternative casing colour of dark gunmetal grey. As a result sales to this sector of the market took off!

Among the latest Apricots to come on to the market is the Qi which has, as with previous Apricots, a certain physical style about it which is rather distinctive from that which went before. Apricot has always been at the forefront of using three and a half inch floppy disks. These are far more robust than their five and a quarter inch counterparts and they certainly lend themselves to being pushed in and out of disk drives with ease and safety. Like the machines which preceded it, the Apricot Qi boasts a small footprint given its capabilities – just 15 inches by 17. It also has a novel approach to the whole question of security (of which more in the next chapter). Traditionally, microcomputers have made use of passwords to secure the information within them. This has meant that in practice people either did not bother to use them or used passwords which were easy for other people to guess, such as their own name or date of birth. The Apricot Qi comes with a 'Qi Card' which generates an infra red beam to unlock the machine and provide a level of access to files which can be pre-determined. This is a most positive approach to the security issue which, even for the small business user, is crucial given the Data Protection legislation which requires personal details stored on computer to be held securely whether they be about employees, customers or suppliers.

Latest state of the art computers such as the Qi offer value for money and the latest in computer features, of which, as we have discussed, the most important are speed and enhanced memory. However, such systems tend to be relatively expensive – over £3,000 for the Qi, more than £4,000 for an equivalent IBM machine. If you are in a start-up business where money is tight the chances are you simply will not be able to afford such sums, especially when you consider there are software and peripherals such as printers to be purchased on top of the basic price for the computer system. The answer then is to go for one of the value for money computers at the low end of the market.

The name which has dominated this scene for the last three years or so has been **Amstrad**. Amstrad have pursued a pile it high, sell it cheap philosophy, supplying what can only be described as amazing computing power for very little money. Most basic business functions should be capable of being carried out by the systems being offered towards the top of the Amstrad range and certainly business in a start-up situation should consider Amstrad as a very positive option. There are one or two pitfalls, however. The first is not to be too bamboozled by the Amstrad policy of selling everything on price. Even at the low end of the market you get only what you pay for and it would be easy to buy one of the cheaper computers only to discover that it is really quite limited for business applications. For example, Amstrad offer one system aimed at

The hardware

regular word processing users for under £500. There is no doubt that it would fulfil most basic business word processing applications admirably. However, as your business grows you would soon find its capacity limiting and its low speed and low memory making it difficult to handle other applications adequately. You will also very probably have to purchase an Amstrad printer as part of the overall package. Such printers are fine for simple work, but totally inadequate for more sophisticated business applications such as high volume mail-shots.

If you do choose one of the cheaper ranges such as Amstrad, the best policy is to purchase a machine at the top of that range and try to ensure that you can add to it other, more suitable peripherals. Even doing that can have its drawbacks. Like other suppliers at the low end of the price range, Amstrad is in the business of shifting large numbers of its machines. The amount of after sales support offered to Amstrad users is nothing like as great as that offered by, say, IBM. But then that is part of what you are paying for when you pay a higher price for an IBM machine. Similarly, in the past Amstrad and other suppliers of computers at the cheaper end of the price spectrum have not been noted for supplying easy to understand manuals for their machines. Indeed, for some Amstrad machines a new industry in writing and supplying alternative manuals has sprung up because the impenetrable manuals supplied with the machines generated a demand for alternative, user friendly documentation.

Another factor worth considering before opting for one of the cheaper ranges is the question of what is going to happen when your computer system needs to grow with your business. It will not necessarily be easy to extend the capacity of your existing machines. They may not be capable of having their memory expanded through the addition of 'plug in' chips. You may not be able to link them together through networking. What is more, if you grow very big you may find that these computers cannot interface with other, more powerful systems. In short, if you think your business will never expand beyond a handful of employees and that you will need your computer for only the most basic of tasks then there is no reason why you should not opt for a cheap one, assuming you have satisfied yourself that it will be capable of fulfilling your current business applications needs. It may well also be advisable to have a

The hardware

cheaper, less sophisticated machine for people (including perhaps yourself) to learn on. Just remember that as people get used to their training machine it is tempting to use it for more than training. It can then be very frustrating if you cannot transfer data stored on disk in one machine to another machine.

Before we leave the subject of computer systems, a word on the use of so-called *home computers*. There are many which claim to offer business type software. Indeed, years ago I can remember learning about spreadsheets using a very basic spreadsheet package on a **Commodore 64** home computer. I also learned the rudiments of word processing on the same machine using a word processing program known as **Easiscript**. You occasionally come across small businesses using such basic home computing systems, but the truth is that they are slow to use and really do not give what one could describe as a polished product. In short: do not be tempted to use such basic computers; you will soon find their lack of speed and memory will badly outweigh any savings in cost to your business.

Choosing peripherals: monitors and printers

The amount of choice you have with peripherals varies depending on how much money you are spending on the basic hardware system. With most systems you will usually have to take the keyboard you are offered. This is no hardship these days: keyboards are very much of a muchness with little to choose between them, so unless you have a need for a special keyboard this will not present a problem. You may be offered a choice of monitor – either colour or monochrome. If you opt for the latter you will have a choice between green or orange lettering on a black background or increasingly popular these days, black lettering on a white background, designed to resemble the printed page. Obviously if you have a colour monitor you can pre-select both the background colour and that of the lettering to something which will suit you. Most spreadsheet programs, when used in conjunction with a colour monitor, tend to specify their own colours anyway. Again, with most systems it is as well to opt for the monitor supplied with the system, although invariably the price of the monitor will be an extra to the system itself – a ploy designed to fool the consumer into believing the

The hardware

system is cheaper than it really is. Do make sure, therefore, that when comparing systems you account for the cost of the system including the monitor of your choice. After all, the computer system itself can be very clever indeed but it is of absolutely no use to you if you have no way of viewing its output!

One point here on monitors. If you are opting for a really cheap computer system you just may be tempted to use an ordinary domestic TV set as a monitor. This is hopeless for business applications, for two main reasons. First, the quality or *resolution* of a domestic TV set is such that you do not get a clear enough definition of letters and figures when they are on the screen. As a result, using a domestic receiver can bring much eye strain to the poor person who is having to word process on the set. Secondly, even the smallest of domestic TV sets is usually too large to fit on the average desk with ease. A purpose designed monitor will usually be built with the space constraint very much in mind.

Of the peripherals which really matter to a business of whatever nature or size the most important is probably the printer. On the printer depends the final image of your computer work. If the image is important to your business, and these days there are very few businesses where it is not, you must elect to buy the best quality printer you can find. It is quite possible to spend almost as much on the printer as you do on the rest of the hardware itself, particularly if you opt for one of the cheaper computer systems. As mentioned earlier the choice is between dot matrix printers, which give a basic print facility with a relatively poor image quality but are able to print out quickly; daisywheel printers, which give letter quality output but do so quite slowly; and ink jet or laser printers, which give good quality output with a range of options on print styles and are capable of printing at speed.

Of the tried and tested makes of dot matrix printers the **Oki** range of Microline printers have proved to be both popular and reliable over the years. They are particularly good with *tractor feed* paper which has sprocket holes down each side of the paper allowing it to be fed into the machine continuously. This can be very useful when printing out long documents such as price lists or detailed quotations. The alternatives are to feed in single sheets one by one, or to purchase a *sheet feeder*. This is a device which stands on top of the printer holding a sheaf of cut paper and, as its name implies, feeds in the sheets one by one. The disadvantage with sheet feeders is that they can cost almost as much as the printer itself. If you are using a dot matrix printer it is best to use tractor feed paper. It is possible to obtain paper of high quality for important letters which is perforated very finely so that the sprocket holes which guide the paper through the printer can be removed cleanly after printing, leaving you with a cut sheet which is almost indistinguishable from an ordinary sheet of paper. If you are doing long runs of correspondence, mail-shot letters and so on, or invoices, it is also possible to have tractor fed paper pre-printed with your own headings just like ordinary headed notepaper. However, for the start-up business watching its cash this will be an added expense that you may wish to avoid. Not only that, even using the double strike facility to produce printed material of Near Letter Quality you will not be able to produce really top-notch printed material. With some businesses this will not be so important. A plumbing business, for example, would not necessarily be expected to produce super quality quotations and invoices which looked as if they had been professionally typeset. If, on the other hand, you are in an image conscious business, public relations, for example, or fashion retailing, you may well feel that as you are selling image the best place to start is with your own business operation. So if you are planning to have a large number of outside communications by way of mail-shots and letters and you are in a business where image counts then you would do well to try to find the money for a better quality printer.

This may mean you will have to adjust the ratio of money you spend on the computer system itself to what you spend on the printer. Remember that even the lowliest of computers can produce good output on a high quality printer, whereas it is not possible to produce high quality output from a top end computer system linked to a basic printer. Before we leave the subject of cheap printers, beware of those which offer printed output on special pressure- or heat-sensitive paper. Some of the cheaper computer systems often come with this kind of printer thrown into the overall package. While such a printer is fine for the odd printout of a spreadsheet, for example, it will be hopeless for other uses, first because such printers are usually very slow and secondly because you are stuck with one type of paper which will be undoubtedly more expensive

The hardware

than ordinary paper and which cannot usually be pre-printed with your own heading except at some cost.

Dot matrix printers will cost in the region of a couple of hundred pounds upwards. The next stage up is the daisywheel printers, which can cost sums similar to the more expensive dot matrix printers but which can also be double the cost if you want to achieve fast results. In addition to the basic printer you may wish to purchase extra daisywheels with different print styles known in printers' jargon as *typefaces* or *fonts*. It is possible with most word processing programs to insert commands into a document to pause the printing process so that you can change the daisywheel if, for example, you wished to show a word or phrase in a different typeface. However, all of this takes time and while it might be a useful facility if you were trying to produce a one-off copy to go, say, to a professional printer it would be a nightmare if you had to do it on a long mail-shot.

Another drawback which dot matrix and daisywheel printers have in common is the amount of noise they make when they are printing. This can be overcome in one of two ways: either by placing the printer within a soundproof hood or by having the printer in a separate room. For most small businesses, the first option adds an unnecessary cost to the business overheads and the second is not usually practical. Despite this, if you are producing just a handful of letters a day and generally using your printer in an intermittent fashion then a daisywheel printer is a good option to choose. Among the tried and tested makes are those produced by **Brother** and **Epson**.

If you want both speed and quality and quiet operation then an ink jet or laser printer is for you. These printers, though costly, give what amounts to state of the art printing technology. Despite their speed of operation they are quiet in use – the amount of noise they generate amounts to little more than a purr! What is more, they take cut sheets of paper which can be loaded singly or in sheaves. It is also quite easy to change the paper quickly. This obviates the need to have specially printed tractor feed paper – ordinary headed paper will do. One drawback with such printers is that the toner cartridges which they use (similar to the toner cartridges used in a photocopier) can be quite expensive, and if you have a heavy print load it is quite easy to exhaust the cartridges quickly. What is more,

The hardware

there is little choice when it comes to replacing these so-called *consumables*: you are tied to those supplied by the manufacturer. You could pay around £15 a cartridge for an ink jet cartridge, up to £100 and in some cases more for a laser cartridge. Although some cartridges claim to give you as much as 10,000 pages of printout you are still talking of prices in the region of a penny a page – more than twice what it would cost using a dot matrix printer with a conventional ribbon. But if you want a quality finish you have to pay for it.

The clear market leaders when it comes to ink jet and laser printers are **Hewlett Packard**. For the small business, their ink jet printer with its relatively cheap replacement cartridge is certainly worth considering if you want a quality finish to your print output at a cost of around £600. Even the most basic of laser printers costs well over £1,000, although prices are dropping as more competition comes on to the scene. It is important to try to assess in advance just how much print output you are going to require. It can be quite damaging to overwork a machine which is not designed for high output. This can result in a poor quality image or complete breakdown of the printer. However, unless your business involves producing print for other people or repeated runs of high volume mail-shots it is unlikely that you will need a large capacity printer. Other makes to look out for in this field are **Canon**, who draw on their vast experience in the photocopier field to produce laser printers of extremely good quality, and **Qume** – a name which has been around some time in the world of dot matrix and daisywheel printers.

One final factor to decide on when buying a printer is page width. Most offer an eighty character column width – a size which is geared to the width of an A4 sheet of paper. It is quite easy to obtain dot matrix and daisywheel printers which print one hundred and thirty two columns. This facility comes into its own when printing out spreadsheets. However, some systems are able to overcome this by using what is known as *compression* to reduce the size of the final printed characters and therefore cram more information on to a page. If you are unlikely to be producing large spreadsheets it is probably better to opt for a printer which has an eighty column width printout capability.

The second-hand option

There is an overwhelming choice when it comes to hardware with new systems being released in the market place weekly. Although still relatively young, the computer industry has already spawned a large selection of computer equipment. Much of it becomes obsolete in a very short space of time; a few months can be a long time in the world of computers. This has meant the creation of a growing market for second-hand equipment. Is this an option for the small business user just about to get into computers? The answer to that is 'Yes' and 'No'. 'Yes', if you stick to well known brand names and can obtain either some kind of warranty from the supplier of the equipment to cover you if it turns out the machine has been dropped and parts of its internal workings have been damaged. 'Yes', if you can have an opportunity of testing it out to check it really does still function. However, the answer must be 'No' if all you are being offered is some obscure machine you have never heard of. The chances are it will be one of the many machines from a myriad of small hardware companies who have been squeezed out of business by the big hardware producers. You may even be offered such machines in pristine condition, brand spanking new in their original boxes at rock bottom prices. Although they might be tempting the best advice to you must be to avoid such bargains. If the firm which produced the machine has gone under or is shaky to whom will you turn if the machine goes wrong? It really is too risky. Remember, too, that even if you go for a well known brand second-hand machine the price you will pay will not reflect any support and this will have to be paid for as you go, as it is difficult to obtain maintenance agreements on such machines. The second-hand market is really for those people who know their way around the computer world and can probably do their own troubleshooting in the event of something going wrong. Alternatively, some people might buy half a dozen machines dirt cheap in the knowledge that they can throw one away if it goes wrong. If you are in the market for just one machine on which your whole business is going to rely you simply cannot take that risk with your business data.

However, if you just want a machine to learn on before you commit your business to a completely new system, a second-hand

The hardware

micro might be the solution. Similarly, if you are a business employing a number of people all of whom need to get hands on experience, then a few very cheap second-hand microcomputers might be a quick way of getting as many pairs of hands on to keyboards as you can. But beware getting carried away by what seems a bargain.

Key points Choosing hardware

- Check you can run the software you have selected
- Look for a computer with as much memory as you can afford
- Do not be hoodwinked by jargon or features you do not need
- Make sure you see the hardware running successfully in another business
- Will you have the physical space for the machine?
- Assess your need for a quality 'image' against the printer you require
- As your business grows make sure your computer is able to grow with it

6

Implementing the system

> **Outline**
>
> This chapter looks at the implementation of the system you have chosen. We examine in detail the important issues of:
>
> - communicating with staff
> - using outside consultants
> - how to actually *buy* the system
> - installing the system

By now you will have a good idea of the sort of software you need to run your business and had a look at the kind of hardware you need to run that software. Up to now it is arguable that you could have achieved this overview of your business and how it could be improved by computerization yourself. However, if you employ staff you will need, if you have not done so already, to go through a period of consultation to ensure that they too get the computer system which best serves their needs. In this chapter we will look at that consultation process. We will also look at how you decide whether to bring in an outside consultant to help you formulate your ideas further and test your objectives against the kind of software and systems you think you might need. The actual purchasing of the computer system is important, too, as it is easy to end up with the wrong kind of deal, so we will look at how you safeguard youself against this eventuality.

Shall we tell the staff?

There was a time when new business systems would simply be imposed on staff with a 'take it or leave it' attitude on the employer's part being very much the norm. The trouble with computers is that it is very easy for staff to 'leave it' and you may not know that they

Implementing the system

have taken that course of action until it is too late. If staff do not fully 'own' a new computer system it will end up being the cause of much frustration to you, the business, and the staff themselves, not to mention your customers. All too often one sees systems imposed from on high which staff find hard to understand and which therefore cause great resentment. One can think of no other area of business operation where there is so much potential for creating problems. The only way of avoiding these problems is to go in for a comprehensive and committed programme of consultation. So how do you set about consultation with staff?

The first point to make is that it is very easy to overdo the consultation process. As the owner/manager of the business you have every right to determine a set of objectives for your business. You also have the right to identify the areas which you think are ripe for computerization, remembering the key criteria of (1) computerizing for profit and (2) computerizing systems which already work well on a manual basis. However, your perception of what is working well and what is not may be at variance with the views of your staff actually carrying out business tasks on a day to day basis. So while you must be the final arbiter and ensure you are not side-tracked from your objectives, it will pay you to ask them for their views.

Initiating consultation

The first practical stage of the consultation process is to set up some kind of forum where views can be aired. In the initial stages it might be best to make this as informal as possible. A sandwich lunch or a suitable occasion at the end of a working day with light refreshments might be a suitable way of launching your computer initiative. At this meeting you might circulate a piece of paper outlining your thoughts on why you should computerize and what you see as the benefits and drawbacks of bringing in a comprehensive new computer system or computerizing a new part of the business. At this first meeting you should be open to as many views as people wish to air. Be prepared for some adverse reaction. Much of this is based on that classic human trait, fear of the unknown. Some of this fear may be particularly evident in older members of staff. Writing in 1987, Sir John Harvey-Jones, the former chairman of ICI, said there was a cut-off age of about thirty-five when it came to computers and the

Implementing the system

fear of them. Below that age, according to Sir John, people tended to have been well exposed to computers, often while at school, and were in the main computer literate. Above the age of thirty-five people had little experience of the machines and tended to find computers daunting and hard to handle. That is not to say that anyone over the age of thirty-five should be written off – far from it. However, a wise entrepreneurial manager introducing computers for the first time will realize that they will probably need to show more understanding for older staff as they will have more ground to make up. Employees in their twenties should have no problems at all as they should have been made familiar with computers at school.

Beware the member of staff who appears in your initial meetings to accept your plans too readily. This is in some ways more dangerous than someone who is hostile to computers. Indifference or blind enthusiasm can mask a failure to grasp the implications of installing a computer system and that could lead in future to misunderstanding and having to go over old ground. It is vital that everyone at that first meeting expresses a committed view about your plans, whether they be for or against them. It is also vital that the meeting sets certain tasks for each individual to perform before the next meeting. These can be fairly straightforward and undemanding; you might circulate brochures of potential hardware and software and ask staff to read them and give their views at the next meeting. You may even ask some staff to go and look at some computer systems in operation at other companies if this is practical. If it is convenient they might also be asked to drop in on a local computer shop and see what is on offer. The essential thing in the first consultative meeting is to get your people to 'think computer'. In this way you will be able to generate enthusiasm for the idea of having a computer on board and as time progresses you should be able to channel that enthusiasm into active support and development of the computer ideas.

The first meeting should last no more than an hour or so. It is important not to over-promote the computer idea too early on. It is a major step for your staff as well as for the business and they need time to get used to it. Remember that the capacity for things getting fouled up will increase dramatically if you try to rush things. Remember, too, that once you have given your staff the chance of contributing their thoughts on computerization you may feel you want to revise your own original views on the computer system planned.

Continuing consultation

You should aim to discuss the proposed computer system with your staff about once a week and review progress. By the second or third week you should be looking for some kind of timetable for its introduction to which everyone can work. It is important that progress is monitored and to that end it would be useful to minute each meeting and ensure that eveyone gets a copy of the minutes. These should not be too detailed: confine them if possible to just one sheet of paper. You as the prime mover should ideally be the one to write the minutes. All of this may sound over-complicated but it is important that your staff feel thoroughly involved in the computer implementation procedure. It cannot be stressed too much that without such involvement it will be difficult to obtain the level of commitment you require if you are to achieve the best out of the system when it is eventually installed.

One way of generating a high level of enthusiasm for the computer system is to take a selection of staff to a computer exhibition. You will need to choose your exhibition carefully and it might be better to attend a 'Business to Business' exhibition rather than one dedicated solely to computers; these latter can appear overpowering with the very latest products from the world of computers vying for prominence. Such dazzling displays of the latest hardware and software will certainly tend to confuse the issue. What is more, at such exhibitions the computers tend to be sold on their features rather than on their business benefits. A Business to Business exhibition will have tried and tested systems using compatible software offering real business solutions. Exhibitors should be able to relate to the kind of problems faced by your staff attending the exhibition and will be able to offer them hands on use of the computer. Apart from the obvious direct benefit of this, the gesture of taking a selection of staff to such an exhibition will greatly improve morale and ought to give them an insight and understanding which will make for a far smoother introduction of the new system.

Once you have narrowed down the options on hardware and software, involving staff in the selection process gives them a good opportunity of testing out the sales patter of the suppliers. Obviously if you have a large number of staff it will not be practical to have them all involved in this. Try to put together a small group which contains

Implementing the system

sceptics as well as computer enthusiasts and which is composed of the people who will be using the computer on a day to day basis; they will be in the best position to have a useful hands on trial of the computer equipment and to pull it to pieces if they have doubts about how effective the system is going to be. Not only that, if there are problems at a later date they, by virtue of their early involvement, will be in a better position to challenge the computer suppliers and get them to put matters right. If you impose a system on them without due consultation any fault which may arise because of the computer under-performing will reflect back on you and your running of the business.

The consultation process should continue beyond the selection stage to cover issues like the siting of various parts of the system – printers, for example. What you need to encourage is the establishment of a relationship between the computer suppliers and your staff. That way you will stand the best chance of getting a good service from them as the system develops.

The outside consultant

We stressed earlier that it is important for you as the owner/manager of the business to be in a position to drive the computerization project forward. It is vital that you do have your finger on the pulse, as it were, but you may feel you simply do not have enough time or expertise to shoulder the problem entirely on your own. In this case you will need a consultant. This is fine as long as you remember one or two possible drawbacks.

The first drawback with computer consultants is that they tend to be experts on computers first and experts on business second. Beware, then, of the computer consultant who has had little involvement in the world of real business. Quite a number of lecturers in computer studies at polytechnics and universities offer themselves as computer consultants for business. Some are extremely good and do a fine job. Unfortunately, many are academically driven and while they may have a deep and intimate knowledge of the latest computer techniques, they may not have anything like the same grasp of business matters. If this is the case they will inevitably be formulating their computer solutions in such a way as to steer you towards having a highly

Implementing the system

sophisticated computer which yet may not be capable of carrying out simple business tasks. Sometimes bright computer students are available as consultants; but again, they will not have the depth of experience to help you evaluate your business needs and translate them into a viable computer solution. Such students can prove useful though, when you have decided on your objectives and need to set up your computer to carry them out. It is often most useful to have a young brain interacting with your new micro and helping older members of your staff make their way around the system. A young student will not be too expensive to employ and will value the experience of working with a microcomputer on real business applications. There is always a large amount of extra work to be done when bringing in a new computer to take over from manual systems and an extra pair of hands on the key board will allow your staff to maintain their productivity within the business.

Of course, approved dealers and suppliers of hardware do offer a consultative process, but naturally you are then locked into that particular hardware. This is fine if you have already decided that you are going down, say, the IBM route or the Apricot route. But if you have yet to decide on the hardware–software mix, how do you get independent advice? One solution is to go to management consultants who have a specialist computer department. These consultants are often attached to the big firms of accountants and so should have a good knowledge of the business issues involved in installing computer systems. On the face of it they will appear expensive, but they are really the only way of getting truly independent advice. They are not allowed, for example, to take a commission from a supplier of hardware or software: their only source of income from the project is the fee you pay them which is calculated on a time basis. Some so-called independent consultants who are not constrained by the rules which apply by virtue of them being part of a larger accountancy firm do take commissions, and although this might mean their fees charged to you might be lessened, their independence is tainted and you must ask yourself whether this is acceptable. In the end you get what you pay for. Skimping on a few pounds at this early stage of the computerization process could well lose you a lot more money later on.

Buying the system

On the face of it, the actual purchase of a computer system may well appear to be the easiest part of the process. In theory it should be. In practice there are many things which can go wrong and you need to safeguard yourself against them. By the time you come to the point when you are actually going to part with money for the computer you should have completed a number of key decision-making processes.

First you should know exactly what it is you are aiming to computerize. Secondly, you should know what software you require and have settled on the hardware options in both computing power and peripherals. You will then be in a position to go to a supplier with a specification of your needs. It is wise to ensure that wherever possible you buy the hardware and software from the same supplier. The reason for this is simple. If something goes wrong with, say, the software, and it and the hardware have been bought from separate sources, you could find that the supplier of the hardware will blame the software and vice versa. It could turn out to be a nightmare getting the matter cleared up. If both hardware and software have come from the same supplier he then has the entire problem in his hands and he has to solve it.

The next thing to do is look at what is on offer at various suppliers. By 'on offer' the last thing that is meant is price. While it is important to keep within your allotted budget for the system, beware of tempting 'cheap deals'. You are going to be with your computer system for some considerable time. It is important you do not spoil the ship for a ha'penny-worth of tar. Far more important is the state of the suppliers themselves. How long have they been in business? Who else have they helped? Will they be able to offer the support and backing you will need when things go wrong? These are perfectly valid questions which in theory ought to be asked of all suppliers. In practice they often go by the board. With most kinds of supplier it is not too critical if the supplier gets into difficulties as you will have already received the goods or services and that is the end of the matter. With a computer system, even the most basic of systems, it is not as simple as that. One way of looking at it is to compare the purchase of a computer with the purchase of a puppy.

You may be familiar with the slogan seen on car stickers: 'A Dog is for Life, not just for Christmas.' It is the same with computers. Like puppies they grow quickly and they need regular feeding and vetting and demand a lot of devotion. And as with everything else, you get out what you put in. You need to ensure that whoever supplied you with the computer system is going to be around to help in future. So have no qualms about asking how long they have been in business; and, more importantly, ask them and yourself some hard questions aimed at assessing how much longer they are going to stay in business. In general, the longer they have been established the better their chances of survival, but remember that a couple of years is a long time in the world of computers so you may have to settle for what appears to be by normal standards a fairly young supplier. If you are opting for a system from one of the better known manufacturers you should be able to take comfort from the fact that they are an approved dealer. If they are they will make great play of displaying stickers and framed certificates to announce that fact to the world. The manufacturers themselves, mindful of their need to maintain their reputations, do not hand out these approved dealerships lightly. They will conduct extensive searches on the financial viability of the suppliers. They will have tested their product knowledge and will also be able to run a series of ongoing courses designed to keep the dealers' knowledge constantly updated. They will also maintain a comprehensive back-up facility to allow dealers to get expert information and help which they can subsequently pass on to you if there is a problem. If something does go wrong and a supplier should fail for some reason, the chances are that a reputable manufacturer will ensure that existing customers are transferred to another supplier and continue to get the support they need.

Maintenance agreements

There is, of course, a price to be paid for all this support and back-up. You will, on purchase of the equipment and software, be invited to take out some form of maintenance agreement to cover any mechanical fault with the system and keep you abreast of new developments. You need to have specified on paper what is included in the maintenance agreement, as they do vary considerably. Some

Implementing the system

are simply extensions of your rights under the Sale of Goods Act covering repairs to faulty equipment. Some limit their liability to the cost of a call out plus so many hours of a computer engineer's time. Some agreements offer the facility of a replacement machine if yours has to be taken away for repair, others do not. It is as well to check on this, for if you come to rely on the computer for day to day operations you will be stranded if you have to lose it for a matter of even a few days. No maintenance agreement can by law *reduce* your rights under the Sale of Goods Act but it is as well to check that you are not being asked to pay over the odds for what amounts to little more than those basic rights.

Maintenance agreements for software differ from those for hardware. Most software packages are constantly being upgraded and will be released on to the market in successive versions. Some software maintenance agreements allow you to receive these upgrades as they occur. They will also entitle you to be informed about any bugs which may have been found in the program by other users. Reputable software suppliers are usually very good about passing this information on to existing users of their software. After all, as discussed earlier, one of the best ways for people to choose a software package for business is to refer to other existing users of the software for their opinion of how well it performs. Software suppliers rely on this referred business, so they will want to ensure that their reputation is not tarnished by faults in the software.

You should recognize that the more sophisticated the maintenance agreement for either software or hardware, the more it will cost. It is still possible to obtain basic back-up for as little as 8 per cent of the overall cost of the system. This fee will be charged on an annual basis and you will be expected to pay the maintenance premium in advance. A more realistic figure to budget for would be around 12 per cent. For prudence and safety you should probably allow 15 per cent of the total hardware and software purchase costs in your system budget.

The purchase agreement

It is vital to ensure that you have a proper purchase agreement drawn up between you and the computer system supplier. You will need to check through the terms of this agreement very carefully to

Implementing the system

ensure that you do not leave yourself exposed in the event of the supplier not performing some part of the agreement. With the most basic of microcomputer systems the agreement will be very simple. You pay the entire cost of the specified hardware and software and walk away with the boxes under your arm. This has its attractions if you are familiar with computer systems and can cope with the setting up and installation of the system. It is certainly the cheapest way of acquiring your system. However, if you are a newcomer to the world of computers or it, as is likely for most start-up businesses, you will not have much time to devote to getting the system up and runnning, you will be better advised to come to an agreement whereby the equipment is delivered and set up on site at your premises. The software is installed and you and your key staff are trained in the use of the system.

This will involve you in much closer specification of your needs and requirements of the system, which is no bad thing. It is not unusual in such arrangements for the supplier to ask for a deposit on placing of the order. This can be as much as 50 per cent of the overall cost of the system. The remainder is payable on the system being installed to your satisfaction. Obviously, such a large purchase will need to be considered carefully and you will also need to look at the impact of the costs on the cash flow forecast of your business. As ever in these cases it is wise to seek advice from your accountant about this. It would also be sensible to let him look over the agreement. He may be able to suggest other methods of paying for the equipment which will not have such an impact on your cash flow.

One such method is leasing. In a leasing agreement a finance company pays the entire purchase cost of the system to the supplier in advance and then charges you as the purchaser regular payments over a fixed period. These payments will include interest charges. The overall cost of the system will be more in the long run; however, you will be in a position to pay for your system as you go and the impact of a big one-off payment will be spread over a longer period – anything from twelve to thirty-six months, or even more in the case of a particularly valuable system. One drawback with leasing is that the computer system and its software remain the property of the leasing company right up to the point at which you make the final payment. So if you did find yourself in difficulties

Implementing the system

with your business you could not sell the system (assuming you wanted to) without the permission of the leasing company, who would expect their outstanding payments to be met in full.

A cheaper way of spreading the costs would be to borrow money from your bank, either on overdraft or by term loan. An overdraft is the cheapest method, with the interest being set at anything from 2½ per cent to 4½ per cent above base lending rate. The disadvantage with this is that you could find yourself paying much more for the system if interest rates soar. (Of course, you pay less if they go down.) With a term loan it is possible to have a fixed rate of interest but this is usually higher than the prevailing overdraft rate. Banks prefer to offer term loans, often referred to as business development loans, rather than extend your existing overdraft facility. Whether you will be allowed to extend your overdraft to finance a computer depends on a number of factors. First and foremost is the case you put to your bank manager for having the system in the first place. He will want to be assured that it is going to benefit the business and not simply turn out to be a white elephant. We have stressed throughout this book that the watchword must be 'Computerize for Profit'. Your bank manager will want to be assured that you have fully understood the need for this and that the business operations you are computerizing will bring in more profit as a result. Another factor in allowing you to have an overdraft extension will be the amount of money already borrowed and the security you have offered the bank. If, for example, you have offered your house as security against the overdraft and it is currently valued at £100,000 your maximum overdraft limit (assuming you have no mortgage on the house) is likely to be only in the order of £50,000. If your computer system is likely to put the overdraft above that limit it is probable you will not be allowed the extra money. Bank managers very seldom wish to take the computer equipment itself as security for the loan as its resale value would be but a fraction of its purchase price – assuming the system could be re-sold at all.

A better way of spreading the cost of a computer system is to see if the supplier will take staggered payments for the system. It is unlikely that they will allow you to take very much credit, as they would prefer you to take advantage of a leasing option. However, depending on how competitive the market is at the time you are purchasing the system, you may be able to have some of the payment deferred. Beware of any suppliers offering their own credit purchase schemes. Often the interest rates being offered are far in excess of those offered by leasing companies. It is always wise to compare the Annual Percentage Rate (APR) being offered and make your judgement accordingly.

The actual cost of maintenance and support is hardly ever raised during the early stages of negotiations for a computer system. As mentioned earlier, you should expect to pay in the region of 10–15 per cent of the price of the overall system – hardware and software combined. From the purchaser's point of view it is better to make maintenance payments on a monthly basis, with a stipulation that you agree to purchase maintenance a year at a time. However, suppliers will usually insist that it is bundled into the cost of the system, particularly if you are purchasing through a leasing company. One area where it will not be possible to have cover under a maintenance support agreement is what is known in the insurance business as consequential loss, that is, those losses of business opportunities or profit which may arise due to a computer malfunction. The suppliers simply will not take that on as a responsibility. That is why it is so vitally important to choose a reliable system backed up by a reliable supplier. What you should be able to stipulate with the suppliers is that in the event of something catastrophic happening to your system which cannot be repaired in a few hours, you are not left stranded without a machine at all. A good supplier will recognize this and should have alternative machines available while yours is being repaired, but do not bank on it. Make sure it is stipulated in the agreement so you know where you stand.

You should also stipulate the delivery date of the system and associated software. This date should be agreed so that it fits in with your plans. Careful thought is needed here. Ideally you should have the computer delivered and installed at a time when business is at its slackest. So if you anticipate a boost in trade for the Christmas season do not agree to take delivery of the computer on 1 December. Try to avoid taking delivery during a holiday period: you will need as many of your staff as possible to be on hand when the machine arrives so they can get the benefit of any training which goes with the system.

What happens if the computer is not delivered on time? In theory, the supplier will have broken his contract and you will be entitled to your deposit back. However, in practice this does not help you much as in addition to the cash already invested you will have devoted considerable management time to liaising with the supplier and it would be foolish to throw all that away unless the situation is totally beyond salvation. Quite often the lack of delivery is due to matters beyond the control of the supplier. The manufacturer does not have the model you require in stock; or the software house is behind in delivering the latest release of your particular program. It is in the interests of the supplier to deliver as soon as he can so that he can complete the sale and pick up the rest of the profit.

A frequent occurrence is that part of the system is delivered but not all of it. If this is the case it could turn out to be a blessing in disguise. See if it is possible to get at least part of the specified function up and running. In this way you will be able to spread the introduction of the computer over a longer period of time and delay payment. On no account, however, should you part with any more money until the full system is delivered and it is achieving all that was set out in your specification.

Installation

One of the first rules to remember about installing a new computer system is that it must be seen as an addition to rather than a replacement for existing office equipment. There have been celebrated cases, particularly in the early days of microcomputers, where the person responsible for the installation of the system became so enthused about the capabilities of the new wonder machine that he threw out all the old office equipment, such as adding machines and typewriters, in the sure knowledge that the new system would calculate and word process away to its heart's content. This was fine until the first program crash (within a week of the computer being installed). Imagine the feelings of the staff, who had been dragged kicking and screaming into the world of computers, when they found they could not perform even a simple task such as typing an address on an envelope.

Where will it go?

The system will take up room and so it has to be realized that space will have to be found, not just for the computer itself and its peripherals but also for the stationery associated with the system. Locate the system in a position which reflects its usage. If it is a small microcomputer then it should be relatively straightforward to locate the machine near the individual who is going to use it most, its most logical position. If word processing is going to be the main use then it must be near those who traditionally do the typing. If you are going to need the microcomputer for spreadsheet analysis then obviously you must have access to it. Locating a computer all really revolves around usage.

Ideally, everyone who has need to use a computer should have a terminal on his desk. In practice microcomputers are still too expensive for most small businesses to achieve this so some element of compromise will be necessary. You should, however, plan to increase the number of micros in your business as it expands and as you prove the profitability of the computer systems you are using.

Having decided on a location for your machine, you will have to think about power supply. All modern computers run on standard thirteen amp ring main supplies. As mentioned previously, you would be strongly advised to invest in an uninterruptible power supply unit, which will be fitted between the mains socket and the computer itself. If there is a mains failure the unit stores enough power for the machine to continue to run for long enough to save any work in progress on the computer, park hard disk heads and shut down the system properly until the power is restored.

Setting up

If you have followed the advice given so far you should take delivery of the machine complete with an installation engineer sent by the computer suppliers. He will take off your hands the responsibility of physically getting the equipment out of its boxes and properly installed. However, you will need to be on hand at all times to consult with him as the installation process unfolds, and above all it is vital that you are there on the first day of the system going in. Most systems suitable for small businesses can be installed within

Implementing the system

one day. If yours is a larger concern calling for rather more complex systems it could take longer. Assuming the initial installation is to take just one day you need to be there so that the installing engineer can liaise with you on passwords and procedures for logging on. Only you can make these decisions, so your presence is indispensable. This is why it is best to specify a firm delivery date with the suppliers and ensure they do their level best to stick to it. However, given the importance of you being on hand when the computer is installed you may find it advisable to block out the days either side of the due date in case there is an alteration at the last moment. It would be unfortunate if you found yourself at the other end of the country on the day the computer system is finally delivered ready for installation.

Not only will the computer system itself have to be physically set up; the software will need to be installed too. The installation process of the software, while usually straightforward, can be complex and involve taking decisions as it is installed about so-called *default values*. A default value is the name given to a function which is automatically carried out every time the machine is operated unless special instructions are fed in to change the value. Such standard values are usually geared to one of the most popular ranges of hardware, typically IBM. However, you may not possess an IBM machine, or even if you do you may find that you want to change some of the default values to fit in better with your way of operating. Default values arise because most software is designed to have maximum flexibility, so that users can have a number of options on the way the software operates; and because *some* alternative must be chosen where there is an option, software developers build into their programs a standard way of operating, based on default values. Default values at their most simple can apply to, say, the background colour displayed on the screen or the width of the printer being used. Some word processing programs, for example, automatically default to a 132 column width printer. If you have an 80 column width printer, every time you print out a document you will have to change the printer width instruction. By changing the default value when the software is being installed you can cut out the need for this extra command when document printing. On their own, default values may not seem significant. However, added together, altering them can represent a considerable amount of

Implementing the system

operator time taken over a period if the values are not correctly adjusted to the needs of your operation. Too many users ignore the facility offered by software programs to tailor these default values offered as standard by the software packages, often at considerable inconvenience to their operations. The reason this happens is that key decision makers are not present during the installation process and the installation engineer is left to get on with the system without any guidance about the business requirements.

Sometimes the engineer forgets to ask about default values. If this happens he must be reminded. In the final analysis it is in your interests to ensure you get the tailoring of the system you require. You must therefore insist that he runs down all the default values for the various packages he is installing and gives you the option to change them.

Doing it yourself

What happens if you have taken delivery of a smaller system under a deal which does not include the services of an installation engineer? You will certainly have saved money on the deal by not acquiring the services of an installation engineer but you now have the responsibility of unpacking the equipment and hooking it all up together. The place to start is with the delivery note, which specifies what kit should have been delivered. This should be methodically checked against the equipment which has actually arrived. There is often a temptation to try to put the system together without first checking that you have all the peices you require. This temptation must be resisted. Quite frequently cables are omitted and you can spend fruitless hours trying to put a system together for lack of the right piece of wire. If you find you are without part of the equipment, you should immediately (after checking to see if anything else is missing) contact your supplier to have the replacement parts sent. It goes without saying that you should not attempt to put the system together without all the necessary parts.

Having established that you have a complete set of equipment the next task is to attempt to link it together. It cannot be stressed too strongly that it is essential to read the manual properly before proceeding further. Too many people read the first section or even the first few pages of the manual, on setting up, and then launch

Implementing the system

into putting the computer system together. Time taken to read the manual through once to familiarize yourself thoroughly with the workings of the system will pay off as you put the system together. Do not worry if you find you cannot take in all the information at the first reading. Not many people can. What matters is that during the initial stages at least you have an overview of the computer system, rather than finding out in depth the workings of just one part of it.

Each system will have different instructions on how the various parts link up. One point all systems have in common is that they will need a power supply. Sometimes there is just one power cable from the mains to the central processing unit and power is then fed out through special connecting cables to the various peripherals – the monitor, the printer, etc. – from there. However, it is usual to have a separate power supply for the printers and in some cases you may find the screen also has a separate supply. In any event, it is vital that the plugs supplying the system are correctly fused. Computers operate on a tiny amount of electrical current which has to be stepped down from the mains via a built-in transformer. However, despite the presence of internal fuses which should blow if for some reason there is a short circuit or in the highly unlikely event of a current surge you will want to be doubly sure that the microchips within the system are protected. For this reason it is imperative that you fit the correctly rated fuse to the mains plug as recommended in the manual.

There will probably be a separate manual for the printer, especially if it is supplied by a different manufacturer. Make sure you have the correct paper in the machine and that the ribbon (in the case of dot matrix and daisywheel printers) has been correctly installed. Look up in the manual how you conduct a test print and run the test. If there is a problem refer it immediately to your supplier. Compared to the computer system itself there are many more mechanical parts to go wrong with a printer and it can be most frustrating if you find yourself with a working computer which has no way of outputting documents because your printer is not working correctly. Checking the printer at an early stage of the setting up operation makes good sense.

Once you have established that the system is correctly linked up and supplied with suitable power sources, it is time to turn to the

Implementing the system

software. Most microcomputers come with a disk based operating system which has to be loaded into the machine every time you switch on the machine. This operation is sometimes known as *booting* the system. You may also be supplied with what is known as a *system generation disk*. This disk contains information which enables you to *configure* your computer so it may be used with a range of peripherals. This configuration will involve changing the default values within the computer itself to fit in with the peripherals. The best example to illustrate the use of the system generation disk for configuration comes when you set up the computer to run your printer. All printers differ in the way in which they react to instructions given to them by the central processing unit. Some will only accept information in a certain way and at a certain speed. If the information is not fed to the printer correctly they can refuse to function at all or print out gobbledegook. All reputable makes of computer recognize this and offer the user the option of configuring the computer so that it releases the information to the printer in a way it can 'understand', by means of the system generation disk. The disk will also help configure the computer to interface with other peripherals such as modems. For most users of a microcomputer the system generation disk will be used only during the installation process. However, for safety it is essential to make a copy of the original disk.

The copying of software is permitted under most software licensing agreements as long as the copies are for security purposes only and are not passed on for the benefit of other microcomputer users. A word of warning here to businesses using more than one microcomputer. The number of copies of the disks you may take will be strictly limited by the licence agreement. It would be unfair and illegal if you made greater use than allowed of a piece of software while still paying the price for use on just one micro. You may not get caught; but if you are (perhaps through some disaffected employee informing on you) you will find it both embarrassing and costly. Fines for software piracy and abuses of copyright are now quite substantial.

Before you can copy any disk you need to have a supply of blank disks. Some may come with the system but it is wise to have at least ten standing by. You will find you will fill them up very quickly. Ensure that you have disks of the right size and specification by

Implementing the system

referring to the manual. Apart from size (either five and a quarter inches or three and a half inches), there is further variation in the way the disks are constructed and you will hear phrases such as *double sided* and *double density*. What these phrases actually mean need not concern you, but it is important that you get precisely the disks specified in the manual, otherwise the computer system may not work. Once you have the correct disk it is then necessary to *format* or *initialize* them. This is a process whereby the computer configures the disk to its way of operating so that the disk can accept information in the way in which the computer wants to deliver it. Different computer systems have different formatting systems. On some it can take quite a time to format each disk – up to a couple of minutes, in some cases. It is not a bad idea to format all your disks in one go so they are ready for use. Alternatively, you may wish to by pre-formatted disks. These are available for IBM and IBM compatible microcomputers and for some of the other leading makes of system.

Once you have formatted your disks, keep them separate from your other disks until you are ready to use them. Follow the instructions in the computer manual to copy your system generation disk and your load or operating system disk. Keep the originals in a safe place, preferably well away from the office environment if this is at all possible. The copies you have made are known as your *working disks*. You can alter them in any way you wish, safe in the knowledge that if something catastrophic happens you still have the originals from which to make new copies. The same principles apply to any new software you buy. It is vital that you do not use the original disks in day to day operations. It is so easy to damage a floppy, and if you corrupt an original disk, even though some software suppliers will be quite generous about supplying replacements it will still take time to have them delivered to you – time which you can never afford in business.

Disk management

Before we leave the subject of software and floppy disks we will consider the question of disk management. Although it is possible to store masses of information on one disk you will find that you will rapidly accumulate several disks as you use your new system. For

Implementing the system

example, it is advisable that each member of staff who needs to use the computer has his own set of working disks. This may not be the most economic way of operating but such proprietorial interest in the computer system should pay dividends when it comes to maintaining staff involvement in the system. However, a difficulty arises when you are looking for a document created on the computer some weeks back and stored on disk. Because of the sheer volume of information on disk which needs to be sifted through, it is often quite difficult to track down precisely the correct document, particularly when there are several disks to be checked. It is therefore vital that you initiate some logical system right from the start of the computer installation process.

The first point to make on this is that each disk should be correctly labelled with details of the information it contains – a copy of the operating system, a software package and so on. It is wise to store documents – letters, reports, spreadsheets, etc. – on separate disks, not on the remaining disk space on the floppy containing the software itself. In this way you can save wear and tear on the disk copies of the programs. It will usually be simply a question of loading the software once at the start of the computer session and then putting the software disk away. If you work in this way, should there at some later stage be a disaster and a disk be destroyed you will lose only the files held on the particular disk in question – not the software too. You should in general aim to have separate disks for spreadsheets, word processed letters, etc. The exception to this is where you are planning to integrate spreadsheets with word processed reports. Each disk should be labelled with the nature of information stored and the date on which storage started. When the disk becomes full the date of the final filing can be added. In this way you make it easier to track down past correspondence. If you are in a security conscious operation you may wish to have separate *security disks*. These disks can be specified for filing documents where extra security is required and can be stored separately under conditions of strengthened physical security, such as a locked safe or filing cabinet.

Implementing the system

Summary

Computer people just love to talk about 'systems'. Their very hierarchy enshrines the word. Virtually every computer programmer longs for the day when he or she can become a systems analyst. It is a very grand name for a pretty mundane, if logical job. In the early days of computers the systems analyst was the person who worked out ways in which a computer could do the range of complicated tasks required. Traditionally, systems analysts would spend several weeks, even months, touring a company, clipboard in hand, getting a feel for the business. They would then spend much time breaking down the complex functions of the operation into a series of much simpler tasks capable of being handled by the computer. In the good old days analysts might uncover all manner of illogical or unsound practices in the course of their investigations, but it was relatively unusual for any great changes to be made. After all, was not the whole purpose of the computerization to improve the efficiency of existing staff and working operations? When you bought a computer, you tended to buy it as a package with bespoke software, and so, with the absence of off-the-peg software, fitting the computer around the business was a much easier task. Psychologically, too, there was less inclination for the champions of a new and growing industry to start telling older and wiser businessmen that their systems were wrong. If they wanted a computer to improve their existing business, then indeed that was the computer they were going to get.

In today's world of small computers for business it is not quite like that: hardware and software still tend to get sold separately, like washing machines and soap powder, although there are signs that that is changing. Hardware manufacturers may well recommend certain software packages, but that does not get the average business user much further; look at the range of soap powders recommended by just one big washing machine manufacturer! The chances are that the average business will have to use one of the existing software packages or have one modified to suit its particular operation. Either choice will certainly be less expensive than the alternative of having software especially written for you – most small businesses simply cannot afford that level of expenditure on software. So despite the overall philosophy of finding suitable software to fit in with your existing business systems, at the end of the day you will have to be prepared to make some compromises in order to use available, off-the-peg software packages.

In a small business you, aided and abetted by your staff, will be playing the role of the systems analyst. When it comes to choosing and installing your computer system you have to ensure that at this crucial stage you stick to your objectives and that you have good comeback on your computer supplier if there are problems with either hardware or software. Above all, you must remember that *you* are in the driving seat.

Key points Implementation

- Fix your objectives
- Consult with staff early
- Write a hardware/software specification
- Do not be tempted by 'cheap offers'
- Purchase both hardware and software from one supplier
- Check supplier's survival factor
- Look for a comprehensive maintenance agreement
- Specify a delivery date in the purchase agreement
- Allocate a suitable location for the system
- Back up disks daily and store copies elsewhere overnight
- Plan adequate space for the system
- Locate on usage
- Aim to have the system installed professionally
- On installation day – be there!
- Tailor default values to your needs
- If you install it yourself – be methodical
- Read the manual through first
- Have plenty of blank disks on hand
- Create working copies of software – don't use original disks
- Set up a disk filing system from the start

7
Housing and security

> **Outline**
>
> This chapter considers the problem of locating the system with particular reference to security:
> - protecting your information
> - safeguarding the hard disk
> - personnel security

In the past finding space for a computer could present considerable problems. They used to take up quite a lot of room, and space is always at a premium in a busy office. These days, with more computer power being packed into much smaller machines, finding room for the computer is far less of a problem. You do, however, need to consider certain elements carefully.

What kind of use?

Much depends on whether the computer is going to be used principally by one person or by a number of individuals; and, of course, on the number of hours each day the machine will be in use. In a small business you may be using it for a variety of functions. You may want it to word process most of the time and be available occasionally for other functions such as spreadsheet analysis or the production of invoices. If you are likely to be using a microcomputer for full scale accountancy functions, it would probably be wise to dedicate an entire system to that function.

While virtually all microcomputers are quite at home on an ordinary desk, in a small business which will probably be able to afford just one microcomputer it may be wise to have it on its own specially designed desk. There are a number of specially designed units available which will hold not only the computer itself but also the printer and its stationery. These units come with castors so they can be wheeled about and placed next to the person currently using the machine. Having such a piece of dedicated furniture also helps prevent the clutter which inevitably accompaines a computer when it is placed on someone's desk. It also stops any kind of proprietorial envy which might arise about who actually has the computer. Needless to say, as soon as a desk becomes a piece of special computer equipment it significantly increases in value. You may feel you would prefer to have an ordinary desk and save money!

If you are using a dot matrix or daisywheel printer you may wish to enclose it in a sound-deadening booth or place a hood over it. This might make it difficult to be transported around the office, however, and as an alternative you may prefer to have a fixed work station area where the computer is permanently located and where individuals may use it as they please. This has another advantage in that you can ensure the environment for the computer work station is all that it needs to be. For example, if you site it in a position where strong sunlight can fall on the screen you will have difficulties seeing the display. Similarly you can create a no smoking/no coffee cup area in the direct vicinity of the computer. Both the equipment and, in particular, floppy disks can be disastrously affected by cigarette ash and spilt liquids.

Security

Security is an issue which is often, sadly, overlooked; but it is becoming increasingly important. As we commit more and more of our business activities to computer it is vital that we protect ourselves and the business from potential damage caused by poor security. If you feel your business is either too small or too unimportant to worry at this stage about security issues, think again. In 1989 a multi-million-pound insurance and securities business in the United States was forced to close down because a fire destroyed its computer equipment and disks full of records of their clients. It was a catastrophic breach of physical security from which the firm was unable to recover. What is more, no amount of insurance could cover the consequential loss of having its computer systems knocked out so comprehensively. Other companies have had real problems when disgruntled employees with access to the computer system cause problems by sabotaging disks and equipment.

Security falls into two categories. The first, already mentioned, is physical security; the second is personnel security. Physical security affects the decisions you make about where you house the computer. In large companies there are very strict rules about this. The main computer system is located in a special computer room and only people who have reason to deal with the computer have access to the room. Obviously it will be unlikely that you will have a dedicated computer room in a small business. However, the principle of allowing access to the computer only to those who need it is a good one. One way of doing this is to ensure you buy a computer which has the facility physically to lock out unauthorized users. All the major manufacturers fit locks to their computers: but it is staggering how often people fail to use them.

Protecting your information

More important is the physical security of the disks. Any business very quickly accumulates masses of information on several disks, much of it privileged, all of it of value. It is vital that these disks are treated like gold. In cash terms alone one disk can represent substantial amounts of money. For example, one five and a quarter inch floppy disk of text would take well over £1,000 worth of operator time just to retype all the information. Add that sum to the commercial value of the information contained on your disks and the figure is much higher. That value is multiplied by the number of disks of information you have.

Disks should therefore be stored securely. Each day back-up copies of key disks should be made, and those disks should be stored elsewhere overnight so that if there is a fire your computer records are not completely wiped out. There are various ways of achieving this. Some businesses deposit their key disks along with their cash in the night safe at their local bank. If you are not in a cash business and this is inconvenient, the back-up disks can be taken home each evening. Some companies invest in a fireproof safe into which disks are placed every night. This is a sensible precaution but there is a strong body of opinion that you should still have back-up copies of key disks as fires can create intense heat which could warp the thin plastic of a disk. Despite the claims of safe manufacturers, you may well feel you would sleep more soundly at night if you knew you had two sets of disks available to your business.

Although microcomputers themselves have become much more rugged in recent years it is still advisable to ensure they have a clean environment to work in. The dangers of cigarette ash and spilled coffee have already been mentioned. Although the hardware is not so susceptible, the disks themselves can be seriously damaged, or *corrupted* to use the computer jargon, by the smallest specks of dust. It is unwise therefore to locate the machine near an open window. However, while modern computers no longer require a fully air-conditioned environment, they do need to be kept at reasonable temperatures, and it is therefore equally unwise to site the computer where it is in the full glare of sunlight. Disks should be held in purpose-designed boxes such as the 'See 10' box which has a special flap enabling you to flip through the disks without bending them.

Safeguards for hard disks

Hard disks can present security problems too. There was an instance where a computer was taken away for repair after a hard disk fault and a new hard disk unit was fitted. No one had bothered to dump off the information held on the hard disk – some 30 megabytes of data. The information included the complete customer list of the company, which was working in a highly competitive area. This list had taken years to build up and was quite detailed, containing information on the size of customer, how much they had spent and so on. Imagine the chagrin when it was discovered several weeks later that the old disk, now repaired, had been fitted to the computer of a competitor which, in addition to getting their machine repaired now had an added bonus of the complete customer list of their chief rival!

Hard disks are quite susceptible to damage and because they contain so much more information than one floppy disk, such damage can have catastrophic consequences. The most common form of damage occurs when the computer is jarred or jolted while the disk is running. The gap between the recording surfaces of the

Housing and security

disks and the read/write heads is tiny – less than the diameter of a human hair. If the machine is jarred and the heads come into contact with the surface of the disk they usually inflict permanent damage and although other parts of the disk surface will remain intact your disk will be unreliable and start to corrupt data stored on it. Similar damage can occur when a computer fitted with a hard disk is moved without the read/write heads first being *parked* by keying in a command to the computer which removes the heads from the recording surfaces. For the same reason it is important to remember not to move a computer with floppy disks inserted. If the machine is to be moved any distance, for example transported in a car, it is advisable to slot in special transportation inserts. These are usually made of soft cardboard and serve to stop the read/write heads moving about. Purpose-designed fully portable machines usually have read/write heads which park automatically when the machine is switched off.

Personnel security

Having dealt with these physical aspects of computer security let us now turn to the question of personnel security. It is important that confidential information is kept that way. A microcomputer provides an easy way to access all manner of information in minutes which would normally take hours to find by sifting through manual records. Each business will have its own view on what is and what is not confidential, but details of employees' pay is an area where confidentiality is a must, not only out of respect for the employee but also to avoid issues arising out of envy and jealousy. You would probably also not wish to have all and sundry leafing through your sales projections and spreadsheets. One way of preventing unauthorized access is through a physical lock, as already mentioned. However, that does not stop a disk being used on a computer to which the user does have access. It is possible to protect the viewing of information through a password system. Again, most of the systems produced by the big manufacturers incorporate a password into the start-up procedures of the computer. The user is required to *log on* by entering his name and password. As the password is typed in no letters appear on the screen so the secret password cannot be read by an onlooker. If the password is correct the user is allowed further

Housing and security

access. Similarly, software and information held on floppy disk can be protected in this way by the use of passwords. However, although such password systems exist they are frequently rendered useless by sloppy practice. For example, people choose obvious passwords such as their surnames or birthdays which could easily be guessed by an unauthorized user. One useful password to employ is your mother's maiden name (a key frequently used by credit card companies wishing to authenticate the identity of a telephone caller wanting a replacement card issued). Obviously in family businesses such a password would be less effective. The actual password should not have any logical connection with either the authorized person or the task in hand. Despite this, one often sees passwords such as 'accounts' or 'spreadsheet' used. One also sees passwords written on to pieces of paper and stuck to the computer – a hopeless state of affairs!

Passwords must be changed regularly. Some management consultants specializing in computer installations advise that they be changed monthly. Much depends on the comings and goings of staff: which leads us to the key personnel security issue. Up to now we have been talking about standard systems put in place to deal with a company running normally. You also have to consider what might happen if your business is involved in a dispute with its staff as a whole or with an individual. Sabotage by disgruntled employees is by no means uncommon and your computer system is open to much abuse. This could be anything from the physical destruction of disks – a favourite trick is to staple them together – to rather more sophisticated interference. An employee who knows computers well can leave what is known as a *time bomb*. This takes the form of a computer message buried somewhere within the software which on a pre-determined date destroys all the computer fields or locks up the computer's operating system, rendering it useless. It is vital that if you have cause to discipline staff, or indeed sack them, you ensure the computer is safe from this kind of sabotage.

Large companies ensure that dismissed staff are not allowed back to their computer terminals and even have them escorted off the premises by security men to ensure they cannot return and wreak havoc. In a small business this option probably will not be open to you. Instead, you will have to rely on ensuring that the staff do not return at a later stage or that, if they do, they can do no damage. It is wise therefore that if you have to dismiss a member of staff you change immediately any passwords which he or she might have used to gain access to sensitive information. You should do this even if the employee is leaving voluntarily. It is not unheard of for staff to return to their old place of work with the intention of lifting a customer list from the computer for the benefit of their new employers. This is particularly dangerous where sales staff are concerned. You must deny them access to the computer. Similarly, you should discourage visits from former employees 'just to see their old workmates'. There is simply too much at stake.

One area of personnel security which is harder to control is where an employee uses the computer to set up a deliberate fraud. A simple way of doing this would be for an employee to have access to the payroll package. It is a relatively straightforward matter for the member of staff to give himself a rise in pay and it is surprising how many months can pass without it being spotted. Another area for potential fraud is computerized order processing. There have been cases where purchase orders have been issued for goods which do not exist. Such collusion between crooked employees and equally crooked suppliers is not peculiar to operations where computers are involved, but a computer system provides enhanced potential for larger frauds of this kind to develop more swiftly.

Of course, this kind of fraud tends to take place in larger rather than smaller businesses; however, it is as well to take precautions against it right from the start. Such precautions include ensuring that any computer operation where cash, purchase orders or invoicing is concerned is checked, and where appropriate a counter-signature system set up. It is vital to split responsibilities so that there is not too much concentration of power in one pair of hands. It goes without saying that strict controls on cheque signing should be in place and reviewed from time to time to ensure the arrangements are still suitably secure.

If you are involved in a business where a high degree of security is required by virtue of the nature of the work you do – for example as a subcontractor in the defence industry – you will be required to demonstrate that you operate far strictre security arrangements than those outlined above. Even if you are not in a sensitive area of business you are required by law under the Data Protection Act to ensure that you protect confidential and personal information held on computer files. Any leak of such information could not only prove embarrassing, it could also cost you money by way of a fine. Good computer security is a must for any well run business, and the best time to put security arrangements in place is at the outset.

Key points   Housing and security

- Locate according to type of use
- Protect access to the computer
- Store disks securely
- Treat hard disks with care
- Use passwords intelligently for effectiveness
- Change passwords when appropriate
- Take precautions against fraud and misappropriation of information

8

Training and monitoring

> **Outline**
>
> Training and monitoring are crucial issues in computerization. This chapter shows you how to:
>
> - organize for training
> - plan for long-term training
> - get paid more quickly
> - improve correspondence
> - improve your business's image

Once your system is in place the crucial issue becomes that of making best use of it; and hence you need to be able to measure its – and your business's – performance. In this chapter we will examine how you can set about this; but first we will look at how you tackle what has been a very neglected area of computer implementation, namely training. We will examine how you maintain a high level of competence among your staff, especially when there is a continual turnover among younger staff.

Training

There are a number of ways you can approach the training of both yourself and your staff. The most obvious is to have them sit down at your computer system and work through the training manuals supplied with each software package on their own. In this way they can learn as they go. If you have invested in something more than a very basic computer system it is to be hoped that you will have negotiated some sort of on-the-job training to be provided by the computer system supplier as part of the overall package. Even if you have, though, this kind of training is, of necessity, at the most basic level and will last at most for just a few days; and this training will take place at the stage when you and your staff are least familiar with the system and will be least able to get the best from what the computer has to offer the business. If you content yourself with just that basic amount of training you will sadly miss out on the tremendous potential the system has to offer.

What do you need?

It is vital that right from the outset you consider carefully what extra computer training can be applied within your business. Such training exists on two levels: first, training directly relevant to the task in hand – a new computer operation aimed at increasing the efficiency of a new sector of your business operation – secondly, training aimed at increasing the general skills of you and your people. These new found skills may not be immediately relevant to the business but they may well come into their own as the business grows and expands. It is, of course, tempting to ignore more general computer training, arguing that it is an expense which can be easily cut when other activities are more pressing. This, though, is a very short-sighted approach. Such is the fundamental change a computer system brings to your business that it is pure folly not to prepare for the continued growth of both your business and the computer operation by ensuring that you and your staff are not held back by a lack of training.

What is required is a mix of training. In the first instance you will need training for your immediate needs and this will take the highest priority. You then want to consider how you are going to tackle longer-term objectives. Taking short-term needs first, try to impress on the system suppliers what your business objectives are and ask them to ensure that the training offered as part of the package addresses those needs. If you are in a very small business you will want to be the first person trained in the way the system operates. You should also work out who else requires immediate training. If you are in a larger business with several employees you will be in the position of having to choose who gets immediate training and who has to wait to get trained on the system. The factors influencing this priority list will include who is closest to the business task being computerized and who it is vital to get 'on your side' to ensure that the new computer system is accepted within the business. Wherever possible you should try to see that the early candidates for training are going to be those who you know will be quickest on the uptake. There is nothing more damning to the introduction of a new office procedure than having it flounder because the first staff to try out the system were not able to make it work.

Organization for training

It is important to make sure you have a well ordered training programme for each member of your staff. The training must be done methodically and you must be able to follow a logical path through the training programme. It is important to ensure, too, that the training is consistent – that is, it must be to the same level for each employee – and to make sure that you have from the outset adequate cover in trained staff so that if one member of staff goes sick or leaves the business you are not left with a skills gap in your computer operations.

If you have more than, say, half a dozen employees in your office then it would be advisable to appoint one of them Training Manager so that the training process can be overseen and monitored. You should then set training goals and objectives with the manager and review progress on a monthly basis. All of this takes time and you will need to budget for this time as you assess the computer project. This is another reason why you should be wary of computerizing everything at once. It is far better to have one element of your business working well with properly trained staff rather than have mediocre performance in a number of areas.

Once the initial training of your existing staff is in hand you should then turn your attention to what happens with new members of staff who join your business. If you are expanding rapidly you could find yourself in a position of having to induct a new person into the ways of your business workings quite frequently. You ought to have an ordered system for this so that each new employee gets the same initial level of training in the system. Even in businesses which are not growing quickly there can often be a high turnover of staff. Some firms, particularly in London and the big cities, are finding they are turning over their junior staff at rates in excess of 25 per cent each year. All of this points to a large investment in training and time just for the business to stand still.

Training over the long term

Turning now to the question of longer-term training, experience shows that the businesses which perform best with their computer systems are those that are able actively to encourage their staff's enthusiasm for the computer system and its potential. To that end it is vital that any long-term training offered is neither intimidating nor boring for the individual. It should be in a form which is easy for the employee to carry through and which serves to inspire positive thinking about the computer system and its capabilities.

One route you could consider would be sending yourself or your staff to computer courses held at your local college of further education. Most colleges now have their own business studies department staffed by people who have been set the objective of providing a service to the business community. Many of these departments are remarkably successful in the way they operate, offering courses which are relevant and effective for business. Some colleges, however, are still offering courses which are more academically based, with far less relevance to the needs and realities of the world of business. Before you commit yourself to such courses ask around of other businesses to see how the college is perceived.

The drawback with further education college courses is that they are tied to attendance at the college at certain times. Usually you will be able to attend classes in the evenings, but in some cases you will have to attend during the day, and this could prove difficult in terms of releasing yourself or your employees from work. If there is a crisis the first thing to suffer is training, and once a class or two have been missed it will be hard for most people to catch up and take the best advantage of what the course has to offer. Also, you may find the fees of further education college courses quite high, based as they are on covering the salary costs of the lecturer, such costs being shared out between anything from ten to thirty students. You may also experience resistance from your staff who might resent the 'back to school' image of attending a further education college alongside much younger students.

All these factors argue very strongly in favour of so-called *open learning*, a growing trend in the world of training, especially for task specific training such as that involving computers. Open learning allows the learner to follow a training course at his own pace and, more importantly to someone working in a small business, at his own convenience. If there is a crisis it is possible to put the training to one side until it has passed without losing out on the training course. If too long a gap has been left between completing various phases of the training package, it is a simple matter to go back over previous work and bring oneself up to the required level to continue the course. Open learning courses, because they are not reliant on a lecturer whose salary costs have to be paid, are of necessity less expensive and represent better value for money. Although they are relatively cheap, modern open learning courses are well packaged and present their material in an accessible, non-threatening way. Because the producers of such courses aim to sell several thousand units they are prepared to pour considerable resources into getting each course as suitable as possible for the needs of the user. Similarly, because they know that in the end it is businesses which will buy the courses and commercial pressure which will make or break the finances there is a much stronger chance of the open learning package being directly relevant to business needs. Far more attention is paid to the way the courses are presented. They usually come in bright packages and often include, in addition to dry printed work books, video and audio tapes to illustrate key points of the course. Such open learning courses are particularly attractive from the employer's point of view in that once purchased the training packages can in the main be used over and over again, thus further reducing the cost per person. Many of the courses on offer can also count towards formal qualifications such as BTec or City and Guilds Diplomas – a further encouragement to the learner.

Among the disadvantages of open learning is that it requires a certain amount of discipline on the part of the learner. It is all too easy to put a course to one side day after day for a time, after which it is ignored completely. In the absence of the regular regime imposed by a college course an open learning package can be quickly sidelined. You can guard against this by encouraging your employees to set themselves clear targets for achieving the work required. If a course requires, say, a hundred hours of study this can

Training and monitoring

quite easily be broken down to ten weeks of studying ten hours a week, or two hours a day, or twenty weeks of studying five hours a week, or an hour a day. It would defeat the objectives of open learning if this became a rigid timetable, but it can serve as a framework within which to complete the course. It is vital you set some kind of timetable, especially if the packages are to be used over and over again for other employees. Open learning does not cut the learner adrift totally: most courses offer a tutoring facility so that learners can have points explained to them and have their progress monitored. Some open learning courses also have examinations which assess just how much the learner has taken on board during the course of study. However, increasingly learners are monitored on continuous assessment, and the emphasis is very much on retained knowledge rather than knowledge learned off by heart to be regurgitated in an exam.

Among the organizations at the forefront of open learning are the Open University and the Open College. The Open University offers not only long, academically orientated courses, often pegged to the academic year, but also more practical short courses. The Open College is aimed more at vocational training for learners in full time employment who want to improve their skills. They offer a range of computer orientated courses which are listed in the Open College prospectus – *The Open Book*. Details of how to obtain *The Open Book* and the Open University prospectus are given in the appendix.

Additionally, the School of Management at the Open University, in collaboration with the Cranfield School of Management, have produced a series of twenty-two modules, under the generic title *The Small Business Programme*, among which is one on computer systems for small businesses consisting of a work book, video cassette, audio cassette and an optional workshop after the module is completed. You will also find a number of organizations offering short courses on specific types of software: there are several available on, for example, how to get the best out of the Lotus 1-2-3 package; but these tend to be aimed more at the executive of a large company who can afford to be released for two days at a time to attend such a course. The small business operation may find it difficult to spare such time and may also find the courses themselves rather more geared to the tasks of the executive charged with producing reports rather than directly to the key issues crucial to running a successful business.

If you have established a successful relationship with your supplier it may well be that they will provide training on a regular basis. This is particularly useful in areas such as word processing where it is wise to book in regular in-house training days so that the trainer can run induction courses for new employees, monitor the skills of existing members of staff and offer guidance and training on new uses of the software. Most modern software programs have capabilities which greatly exceed the level to which they are used. Often the extra facilities available are not relevant to the business but a trainer coming in from outside can often offer useful time-saving pointers to better exploitation of the system. It would be worth negotiating a block booking for a series of training days or half days over a period of months. That way, although you may not be sure of your precise training needs as the year progresses, you will ensure that you do not overlook the training element of your business operation. In addition to your fixed training days you will be able to add on extra training, through open learning, off the job seminars or local college courses to suit your needs.

Monitoring

Monitoring the progress of your computer system is one area which invariably tends to get overlooked. There tends to be so much concentration on getting the computer in and up and running that it is just assumed that it will be an improvement. However, given our stated aim of computerizing for profit, we have to have some way of measuring how successful the computer system has been at improving our business.

To be able to monitor successfully you will need some kind of benchmark against which to measure performance. The most obvious one is profitability, the so-called bottom line. It can, though, take some time, perhaps years, to see improvements on the bottom line, and even if you do there may be a number of factors responsible for the improved profitability; in many cases it will be hard to separate out the computer element of the improvement. When monitoring computer performance it is far better to identify those factors which you know contribute towards increased business efficiency. Let us look at a few.

How quickly are you getting paid?

One of the quickest ways for a business to make more money is for it to be paid more quickly. Depending on the business there will be a specific time in the sales cycle when you ask for your money. This varies from business to business. It could be in advance of delivering the goods or service, when the goods are handed over or several days or even months after delivery. Obviously, if you are in a cash business – selling apples off a barrow for example – you will be getting instant payment for your goods and there would be little scope for increasing the speed with which you are paid. That is perhaps why you do not see many computers on fruit barrows! However, increasingly business is done on a non-cash basis. You are expected to issue invoices and offer some form of credit terms to your customers.

Normal terms are thirty days from the date of the invoice. The trouble is, despite this convention there is no legally enforceable way of ensuring that your customers stick to your terms, and if the stated terms are thirty days many will take much longer, particularly if they are big companies who invariably blame the payment cycle of their accounts department and/or their computer systems for late payments. This is itself a difficult enough state of affairs, but small businesses often add to their problems by neglecting to issue invoices promptly. This tardiness can badly affect any business but in a rapidly growing concern with increasing sales it can spell disaster. It costs money to fulfil each sale and if you have an ever-increasing level of sales you will need to find that money from somewhere if it is taking time to get paid. Eventually your borrowing powers will run out and you will be *overtrading*, a term defined earlier describing a business which takes in more raw materials to service an increasing level of sales and cannot afford to pay its suppliers on time. In short, overtrading occurs when your purchases outstrip your borrowing powers and you are relying on the goodwill or extended credit of your suppliers. It is a highly dangerous position for a business to be in, and many apparently booming companies have gone under through overtrading. Using a computer to generate invoices can help prevent this, but only if you combine the computer system with good management practices. You should have frequent computer runs for producing invoices, scheduled in at appropriate intervals – monthly, weekly or even daily. If you are in a service business or one where stage payments are being made you must ensure you issue invoices in accordance with your stated terms. If you do not, and delay issuing invoices, you will often find that your customers will view this as a sign of weakness and take even more time to pay. The same applies to issuing end-of-the-month statements of accounts and follow-up reminders. If they are issued promptly and you chase them up assiduously your customers will realize you mean business and expect to be paid on time.

Before you measure the success of your computer system in speeding up your invoicing you must quantify how efficient you are at present without the computer. Part of the planning process for installing a computer system should consist of an assessment of how well you are currently doing. So make provision to identify the number of days it takes, on average, first, to issue an invoice once the job has been done, the service supplied or the goods delivered; and secondly, to get paid. Ideally you should monitor for at least a six-month period, but certainly no less than three months, so you can get a feel for the efficiency over a reasonable length of time. Once the computer is installed and you are using it to issue invoices, continue the monitoring and identify any improvement. Of course, there might be no improvement and the situation may worsen because of unforeseen problems with computer invoicing. These problems will remain unseen if you have no way of measuring invoicing efficiently against previous performance. If you are monitoring the situation you should be able to see glaring problems within a month or so and, it is to be hoped, do something to address the situation.

Is correspondence swift and smooth?

If you are generating a lot of correspondence you will want word processing to improve the operation. Much of the effectiveness of a word processing system lies in the greatly improved images presented in the printed work your business produces. Measurement of how much improvement is achieved here will of course be subjective and vary with opinion. Even if your customers are united in telling you how much they approve of your enhanced image, it will be hard to define in quantifiable terms how much that improvement has increased your profitability, and even harder to ascribe such improvements to the word processing operation. What you can measure, however, is the increase in the volume of documents you produce each week. Which documents are significant in terms of business profitability will vary. If you are in the business of supplying a service where it is customary to quote for each job on a separate basis, such as plumbing, painting and decorating or landscape gardening then the quicker you can get your quotation out the quicker you will get a response. There will be a ratio of the number of quotations sent out to the number of successful jobs confirmed. It stands to reason, therefore, that the more quotations you get out, the more likely you are to do more business. If you are in some kind of consulting business where you have to produce reports for clients, it is unlikely that you will get paid in full until your clients have received the final report on a project. Word processing should help you speed up the report drafting operation, enabling you to issue your invoice for payment earlier.

If you use word processing in conjunction with a database and mailmerge facility you should be able to mail potential clients more frequently, inviting them to buy other products or services. Again, this is measurable by the number of mail-outs you make. You can make a crude estimate of the increase in mail-out activity by examining your weekly or monthly postage bill. Once again, you will only be able to make use of such information if you have a benchmark against which you can measure your mail-out operation, so it is vital you have previous mail-out figures covering the immediate past period before the introduction of the computer system.

You may remember that when we discussed the whole nature of word processing programs it was stated that you would be highly unlikely to save any staff by introducing word processing programs. This, therefore, is not a valid measure for monitoring. If anything, you may need more staff to cope with the increased flow of paper produced by the word processing operation. Mail-outs, for example, still require someone to stuff the envelopes – a costly process in terms of time. You may find in the initial stages that you become less efficient with your printed output on computer because of what is known as the 'perfection' factor. It is so easy to correct an incorrectly spelled word in processed documents by correcting on screen and reprinting the page rather than letting the document go out with a written-in correction as you might do with a conventionally typed document, that serious delays can result. This is perhaps to be expected initially. However, if such practices persist you will have to look at other methods of making sure the documents are more accurately put together in the first instance, or even consider instigating a rule which allows documents to be hand corrected rather than be sent back for more word processing.

Image payoffs

Other aspects of computerization are harder to monitor. If you are using computer graphics for producing graphs and charts in reports it will be hard to see any direct benefit to the profitability of the business. However, much of the driving force behind such computer programs lies in an element of 'keeping up with the Joneses' and you may find you are computerizing these areas just to stay in line with or ahead of the competition: if you did not install such systems you could find business falling off. Direct measurements of efficiency in this area are hard to make, and you may have to settle for taking some decision on 'gut feeling' alone.

It is a different story, however, if you are using more complicated software, say specialized computer graphics packages to help you design work for your clients and customers. A carpenter might well use specialized computer graphics to draw up a number of options for fitted kitchens. He could measure his efficiency by comparing the number of days it takes to get the drawings out compared to his old manual methods, the number of options he can give customers and the conversion rate of quotations to actual jobs. All of this will give him a feel for the efficiency of his computer operation.

Monitoring requires careful thought to ensure you measure the correct factors which will truly indicate to you just how well your business is doing. Ideally, there should be no more than half a dozen numbers which are easy to collect. Any more, and the chances are you will soon tire of having to collect the figures and the monitoring process will go by the board: and if you elect to ignore monitoring, how will you ever tell whether your money has been well spent on your computer system? Moreover, how will you decide how to make future decisions about new areas to computerize or upgrading of your existing computer systems?

> **Key points** Training and monitoring
>
> - Organize proper and regular training for all
> - Look at the potential for open learning
> - Establish monitoring factors *before* you computerize
> - Monitor factors which can easily be measured
> - Review performance regularly
> - Take action early to put things right

9
Expansion

> **Outline**
>
> This chapter examines the role of computerization on your business expansion. It considers:
>
> - the need to plan for growth
> - spotting future trends
> - networking
> - electronic mail
> - looking to the future

Once you have your computer system up and running you should find that very quickly you will want the system to tackle more and more of your business activities. We have discussed in previous chapters the necessity for careful planning throughout any computer initiative. It goes without saying that any expansion programme requires the same care and attention to detail. In this chapter we will look at some of the issues involved with expanding your system to take in more of your business activities. We will also examine some general areas of computing into which you might wish to expand, such as electronic mail and networking.

Knowing when and how to grow

Sooner or later you will want more from your computer system. When it is first installed the usual feeling is one of being totally overwhelmed by the system, sometimes coupled with a hopeless feeling of wonder at how you will ever master its complexities. In reality, very few businesses introduce a computer without finding that within a year the demands of the system outstrip its capabilities. If you have gone about the choice and implementation of your initial system in a methodical and systematic way, you should be building on the established success of your computer system. The question then remains: how do you enhance the power and versatility of the system without endangering all the good work you have already achieved in the business?

The choice of paths for expansion within a computer operation can often seem bewildering. Sometimes, though, the true course is obvious and will be driven by the facilities offered by your existing software. For example, if you have an accounts package you will have introduced it module by module. With the advice of your accountants, you will install over a period a series of modules which gradually take the time consuming drudgery away from the business of creating purchase and sales ledgers, running through to trial balances, leaving an easy to follow audit trail which ought to save some of the chargeable time of your professional advisers. You will have worked out in advance the order in which to introduce the modules. This is in itself a useful expansion progression.

Many businesses do not need accounts packages because their size does not justify the time involved in setting them up and running them. If yours is such a business, do not be tempted to introduce computerized accounts just for the sake of it, if you have had success with other areas of computerization such as word processing and spreadsheets. Once again, the emphasis has to be on cost effectiveness and the golden rule of computerizing for profit. There is no obligation on any business to computerize everything in sight. If you think you have gone far enough with your computer operation, stop. Do not waste time which could be better spent on other aspects of the business.

Let us now focus on where you might want to expand. You are more likely to want to expand in areas more closely related to the profit building side of your operation rather than the money counting side of it, important though that is. Here again, the watchword must be to expand into areas you know will bring added profitability. Such areas should be associated with those which are already computerized and should be, wherever possible, a natural extension of the computerization process. For example, if you have word processing on stream you should look at creating a database of customers which interfaces with it. If computerized invoicing is working well within

Expansion

your business, look at the possibility of collating the information contained in your list of invoices to produce reports which tell you what the trends are in sales. Such reports produced perhaps on a monthly basis will help identify areas which need attention. If you are in a business where you have substantial holdings of stock you will be able to see which are the slow moving lines, which items tend to be sold together. You can use these reports to have a better informed marketing plan aimed at persuading your customers to purchase more items of high margin. Similarly, if you are retailing you can use such information to help you merchandise such items together with other products you know you can sell on the back of them.

Expanding the computer operation is fine as long as you do not fall into the trap of making your computer operation so integrated that each part depends on some other operation. This can happen on two levels. The first is that of the sheer physical restrictions which arise over access to the system. Only one person can use a keyboard at any one time. If the machine contains highly integrated programs designed to produce complicated management reports, it may well deny access to usage more directly relevant to profitability. Before you get too complicated, consider investing in more hardware so that you can spread the use of the computer system more widely within the business. It may also be more efficient to have your new programs running on compatible but separate stand alone machines.

Future trends

There seems to be no let-up in the trend towards more and more powerful computers. This increasing computing power will lead to even more sophisticated programs. It should also lead to more user friendly systems which employ the extra computer capacity to store software to help the user through a program. It will also enable faster retrieval from database systems and offer an ability to enter data in a far more random manner than before.

If you have bought one of the better known makes of computer system the chances are you will be able to upgrade or expand the memory of your machine by purchasing new printed circuit boards containing more memory chips. Most modern processor units are designed with space to insert these extra boards which can add to or in some cases replace existing circuitry. This has the advantage of expanding the capabilities of your existing hardware without involving you in the expense of buying completely new equipment. You can also use such plug-in boards to increase the speed of your machine.

Networking

Networking will become increasingly common over the next few years. This is the ability to link computers together so that information can be sent between them. Networking is particularly useful in a situation where you have information which is constantly being updated and altered. For example, you may have a business where you need to check availability of products in stock. This information will obviously have to be made available to your sales staff. You will also have to have the information available to your office staff so that reordering can be carried out. You could have a system whereby a salesman on the road can call up your office computer and access the inventory files while he is with a customer. He can then see what stock is available and reserve it for his customer if required. This can be achieved remotely from the customer's premises by using a small portable computer with a modem which links into the office computer via the telephone. In this way the information is instantly relayed back to the office and prevents that particular item of stock from being allocated to someone else. It also has the advantage of greatly speeding up the despatch of the item and subsequent invoicing. This increased efficiency ought to lead to more profit.

Even if you are in a service business networking can still be of use to you. Supposing you are in a small contracting business, say painting and decorating. You are out selling your services and inevitably a potential customer wants a quotation for the work. You can use a portable computer to work out a quote there and then by feeding in the dimensions of a building to be painted, the type of paint, etc., and arrive at a price for the job. With the right software your computer will also give you the number of man days required to do the job. The next task will be to give your customer an idea of when the work can be carried out. This is where networking in its most basic form comes in. If you are on your own it will simply be a matter of linking up your diary. However, if you employ people, and more to the point, if you have a partner who is also out on the road bringing in business, you will have to take account of holidays and other work which may be coming in at the same time as you are clinching the deal with your customer. By networking via a modem into your base computer you can instantly see when there is an available slot for the work to be carried out. The main computer will tell you about both time-scale and availability of staff. The computer will have holidays logged in and will be able therefore to give you the first available slot which matches your needs in both manpower and time. Because you are able to reserve the slot there and then you can ensure that your partner or other members of staff will not overbook the period. In this way you can rely upon having a constantly updated diary and work schedule. Clearly, this will improve your business by enabling you to get quotes out quicker. The quicker the customer receives the quote, the quicker he can give you the work and the faster your business can progress.

Networking also has applications in the field of desktop publishing. Within an office, or indeed an entire building, documents can be passed around the business to be approved and improved on with the aim of enhancing the ultimate image of the document and ultimately that of the business. Networking in this area offers the first real opportunity of reducing the amount of paper in the office by cutting out the need to print out several drafts of documents before the final approved version.

Successful use of networking relies on two key principles. First, a much more open approach to the sharing of information. Greater amounts of information will be available to many more people. Secondly, there should be a greater sense of responsibility about how this information is dealt with. People within businesses need to be encouraged to think carefully before they amend information held on central files. Clearly this is an area for advanced training in the various judgements required for dealing with the information.

You will also have to think much more carefully about the use of passwords. A disaffected employee can wreak havoc if he is allowed unbridled access to a networked system. Another drawback to networking is that viruses and software bugs can spread very quickly through your entire system. You will have to be even more vigilant about not allowing unauthorized software to be used on your system.

Electronic mail

Electronic mail tends to be of most use to large businesses and the executives who work within them. It is particularly useful to businessmen travelling abroad. Using a portable computer and modem they can access their electronic mailbox at any time of the night or day and pick up messages left for them. They can of course also send messages to other electronic mailboxes in the same way. This is particularly useful when people are operating in various time zones.

How can electronic mail be of use to the smaller business? This really depends on the type of business you are in. If you are keen to market to people who have electronic mailboxes, that is, normally, executives in larger companies, you could do it by sending out your marketing messages by electronic mail. That way you know the chances are it is going to be read by the right person. There is still sufficient novelty value in electronic mail to make it compulsive viewing for the bored executive. There is also a sense of urgency surrounding electronic mail compared with conventional hard copy mail. Electronic mail can also be cheaper, especially if you are sending short documents. It is clearer than faxed messages which, although used increasingly, still suffer from the problem of transmission quality. If you set up your computer for electronic mail by subscribing to one of the various electronic mailbox systems such as British Telecom 'Gold' you will receive as a subscriber much useful information about other subscribers, together with their mailbox numbers. It is for you to decide whether you could take advantage of this information by reaching a market electronically which may have proved harder to crack by conventional means.

Be wise, be wary

Before you decide to expand into other areas of computing, make sure you consolidate the areas where you have already achieved success. On no account jeopardize what you are already doing for the sake of expansion. Think very carefully about bringing in extra hardware rather than overloading the existing system with more software. Remember that it is keyboards which are the limiting factor – only one person can operate a keyboard at any one time. It will be frustrating if the computer system is carrying out one task and you want to do something else. It is far better to expand with a separate but compatible system and link the computers up if appropriate at a later stage. Above all, do not neglect training as you expand. You will still need your staff to be up to speed on your existing system. You must ensure that any new systems do not confuse them and undermine their existing computer work.

Thoughts on the future

Most business tasks are now capable of being tackled by the thousands of software packages on the market. Still the key software tools are the most basic ones such as word processing and spreadsheets. In essence they have changed little in recent years, but of course are constantly being enhanced in their speed, efficiency and ease of use. There has been a steep learning curve over the last few years in the software industry and most businesses ought to be able to find what they want to help their business increase its efficiency.

The saying goes that there is little new under the sun and that is increasingly the case in the computer world. However, one revolution being eagerly awaited is the development of a cheap and reliable *Optical Character Recognition* device or OCR. This will enable text to be put into a computer system by scanning it with a photocopier-like device, creating large savings in time over conventional keyboard entry. Such devices are already being produced but are not generally available at a price most small businesses can afford. When they are, they could provide a real breakthrough in computer efficiency.

There are many wonderful and exciting developments coming through, but these are initially of interest to computer people themselves rather than to the business user who has to see the real benefits of any system. There is enough business software available for most applications of general interest to the smaller business. Word processing programs abound and there are scores of spreadsheet programs. Stick to the simpler programs which have been tried and tested over time. Above all, remember that to succeed with computers you must **computerize for profit!**

Key points Expansion

- Expand carefully
- Do not jeopardize existing computer operations
- Consider more hardware, not more complicated software
- If you have computerized enough, stop!
- If you network remember the security issues
- When expanding do not neglect training

Appendix: Where to go for further advice

There is no shortage of advice in the computer world. The trouble is that much of it comes from vested interests keen on promoting one system over another. There are, though, some independent sources of information. Most local polytechnics and colleges of technology and further education have computer departments and it would be well worth making contact with them in the early stages of making plans for a computer system. Other organizations to try are listed below.

The National Computing Centre

Bracken House, Charles Street, Oxford Road, Manchester M1 7BD. Tel.: 061 228 6333

The NCC has branches in London, Birmingham, Bristol, Belfast and Glasgow. They can also give you the name of the nearest Microsystems Centre. The organization is backed by the Government and Industry. You can subscribe to the organization or simply take advantage of their various advice packages.

Federation of Microsystems Centres

Supported by the Department of Trade and Industry and co-ordinated by the National Computing Centre, there are fifteen specialist Microsystems Centres around the country. They hold workshops and seminars and their staff offer guidance and hands on experience free of any commercial pressure.

Here is the full list of Microsystems Centres:

Birmingham Microsystems Centre
Business Support Centre, Wolverley House, 18 Digbeth, Birmingham B5 6BJ. Tel.: 021 631 4940 (Nick Tempest, Sharon Michel)

Business Resources Centre
Bolton Institute of Higher Education, Deane Road, Bolton Lancashire, BL3 5AB. Tel.: 0204 28851 (Jim Howard)

Bristol Microsystems Centre
Bristol ITEC, St Anne's House, St Anne's Road, Bristol BS4 4AB. Tel.: 0272 779247 (Robert Spencer)

Appendix: Where to go for further advice

Cheltenham Microsystems Centre
CLOSCAT, Park Campus, Merestones Road, The Park, Cheltenham, Gloucester GL50 2RR. Tel.: 0242 532054/5 (Joy Merrell, Dr Noel Meeke)

Dorset Microsystems Centre
Ground Floor, Holland House, Oxford Road, Bournemouth BH8 8EZ. Tel.: 0202 298622 (Brian Weeks)

Dublin Microsystems Centre
College of Commerce, Rathmines Road, Dublin. Tel.: 0001 970666 (Charlie Pritchard)

Greater Manchester Microsystems Centre
Salbec House, 100 Broughton Road, Salford M6 6GS. Tel.: 061 736 8921 (Barry Clayton)

Hampshire Microsystems Centre
Basingstoke Technical College, Worthing Road, Basingstoke RG1 1TN. Tel.: 0256 54141 (Mike Newns, Dave Lehane)

London Microsystems Centre
11 Clarke Path, Oldhill Place, London N16 6QE. Tel.: 01 802 1017 (David Bull)

Newcastle Microsystems Centre (Federation Administration Unit)
3 Heaton Road, Newcastle upon Tyne NE6 1SA. Tel.: 091 276 6288 (Judith Parker, Trevor Cornwell)

Norwich Microsystems Centre
Ivory House Site, All Saints Green, Norwich NR1 3NB. Tel.: 0603 761076 (David Evans, Ron Bates)

South Yorkshire Microsystems Centre
Sheffield Science Park, Cooper Building, Arundel Street, Sheffield S1 2NR. Tel.: 0742 738258 (Neil Goodenough, Carol Kenyan)

Strathclyde Microsystems Centre
Technology & Business Centre, Paisley College of Technology, High Street, Paisley PA1 2BE. Tel.: 041 887 0932/1241 (Brian Cross, Roger Massey)

Washington Microsystems Centre
Micro Technology Centre, Armstrong House, Armstrong Road, District 2, Washington NE37 1PR. Tel.: 091 417 8517 (Martin Haywood, Roger Silk, Paul Kitching)

West Yorkshire Microsystems Centre
Leeds Polytechnic, Queenswood House, Beckett Park, Leeds LS6 3QS. Tel.: 0532 759741 (Tony Riding, Noel Akers)

Appendix: Where to go for further advice

For details of 'open learning' and other training options, contact:

The Open University
The Central Enquiry Service, The Open University, PO Box 71, Milton Keynes MK7 6AQ. Tel.: 0908 635231

The Open College
101 Wigmore Street, London W1A 9AA. Tel.: 01 935 8088.
The Open Book is obtained by ringing 0253 865757.

The Data Protection Act
Any business that holds records of personal data on individuals in computer files is required to register immediately with:

The Data Protection Registrar
Springfield House
Water Lane
Wilmslow
Cheshire SK9 5AX
Tel.: 0625 535777 for enquiries

Glossary

back-up The copying of disks as a safety precaution against information being lost through accidental erasure. Some computer systems do this automatically, with others you need to remember to 'back-up' at regular intervals.

bespoke A computer program written or 'tailored' especially to fit your business needs.

bit Basic unit of computer capacity. It takes eight bits to make one *byte* – the amount of computer space required for one character.

bug An error in either the software or hardware of a computer system.

byte Eight *bits*. One byte represents one character. The capacity of a computer system is usually measured in *kilobytes* (thousands of bytes) or *megabytes* (millions of bytes).

CAD or computer aided design The use of computers to aid design by the use of computer graphics, modelling, analysis and simulation.

CAM or computer aided manufacturing The use of a set of computer instructions to run a manufacturing process.

compatibility The capability of two computer devices to be used in conjunction with each other. All links in the computer 'chain', both hardware and software, must be compatible if a system is to work properly.

CPS Characters per second. A measure of printer speed.

CPU or central processing unit The 'brain' of the computer system where information is handled and sorted.

crash When a program refuses to continue. It usually means that the program has to be reloaded and work in progress can often be lost unless it has been saved or backed up.

cursor The light indicator on a visual display unit (VDU).

daisywheel The name given to printers which 'impress' letters on to a page from an interchangeable plastic wheel. Daisywheel printers give a high quality finish but are quite slow.

database Data held in a computer system which can be accessed and

Glossary

sorted in a number of ways. Useful for maintaining mailing lists and customer accounts.

disk drive A device into which a floppy disk is inserted; it can read the content of the disk and record or write new information on to the disk.

documentation Printed instructions accompanying all hardware and software.

dot matrix A printer which forms characters and graphics from a series of dots. Dot matrix printers are fast but they often sacrifice quality.

double strike An instruction given to a dot matrix printer to print over each character twice, enhancing the finished look of the text.

enter To put information into a computer system.

floppy disk A magnetic disk, usually between 3½ and 8 inches in diameter, which holds computerized information.

format The organization of data in a pre-determined order. A new disk has to be 'formatted' before it can be used with the computer system in question. The word is also used in word processing to describe the appearance of the printed page.

function keys Keys which perform often quite complicated sets of instructions at the touch of just one button. Some keyboards, as in the case of word processors, have function keys for specific tasks such as *insert* and *delete*. Function keys can be altered to suit individual needs.

hard disk A magnetic disk with very high storage capacity. Sometimes known as a 'Winchester disk'.

hardware The various pieces of equipment, central processor, keyboard, printer etc, which make up the computer system.

icon A picture displayed on the screen which represents a function, for example, a pencil invites the user to 'draw' a picture. A filing cabinet represents the function for saving a file.

interface The point at which two devices in the computer system meet.

kilobyte A thousand bytes, often abbreviated to K.

laser printer A high speed, high quality printer which uses laser light technology.

mailmerge A means by which a standard letter can be customized to a mailing list for mail-shots, circulars etc.

Glossary

mainframe A large high capacity computer capable of undertaking highly complex computing tasks and carrying them out in a relatively short space of time.

megabyte One million bytes, Mb.

modem A device enabling computer information to be sent down a telephone line.

monitor A screen on which computer information is displayed. Sometimes known as a Visual Display Unit or VDU.

mouse A small device which is rolled around the desk top to control the movement of the cursor on the display screen. When the cursor is pointing at the required function on the screen a button on the top of the mouse is pressed and the function implemented.

networking The linking together of several computers, either within one office or one building (Local Area Network System or LANS) or over larger distances (Wide Area Network System or WANS).

OCR or optical character recognition A device which scans a printed page and inputs the text into the computer system so it can be displayed on a monitor ready for editing in the normal way.

operating system The means by which a computer system carries out its routine functions.

program A series of instructions which tell the computer system to perform various tasks.

RAM or random access memory The space on silicon chips within the central processor where information is stored and accessed at random.

ROM or read only memory Silicon chips within the central processor which store permanently instructions for the operating of the computer system.

scroll The word processing term used to describe the rolling up or down of a page of text on the screen.

software Information in computer language which instructs the computer system on how to operate (operating software) and perform a variety of tasks (applications software).

VDU or visual display unit The screen on which computer information is displayed

Winchester disk Another name for hard disk.

Glossary

word processing A sophisticated system for typing, editing, storing and printing text.

work station A terminal (keyboard and monitor screen) with access to computer facilities.